If There Is NO GOD

Meditations On Believing

Daniel M. Keeran

Counsellor Publishing
Vancouver
British Columbia, Canada

Copyright © 2008 by Daniel Keeran.

If There Is No God: Meditations On Believing
by Daniel M. Keeran.

Printed in the United States of America.

All rights reserved solely by the author. The author guarantees all contents are original and do not infringe upon the legal rights of any other person or work. No part of this book may be reproduced in any form without the permission of the author. The views expressed in this book are not necessarily those of the publisher.

National Library of Canada Cataloguing in Publication

Keeran, Daniel M., 1947-
  If there is no God : meditations on believing / by Daniel M. Keeran.

Includes bibliographical references.
ISBN 0-9694155-4-0

1. Belief and doubt--Moral and ethical aspects. 2. Belief and doubt--Meditations. 3. Christian thics—Meditations. I. Title.

BT103.K44 2004   241   C2003-907270-3

This book is dedicated to my mother and father who nurtured me, to my loving wife and children, and to all who face the challenges of believing.

Table of Contents

Introduction — 9
How To Use This Book — 12
A Word of Caution — 13

Meditations On Believing — 15

1. Man is only physical and has no soul or spirit.
2. People have no greater value than other life forms.
3. There is no right and wrong, no morality, and no integrity.
4. Human destiny belongs to the clever and strong.
5. The concepts of worth and value do not exist.
6. There is no love, and love is no better than indifference.
7. Life is no better than death.
8. There is no difference between life and non-life.
9. There is no hope beyond death, and death is the end.
10. There is no purpose or design in the universe.
11. Peace is not better than war.
12. Humans are not responsible for the care of the earth.
13. Freedom is not better than slavery.

14. There is no beginning and no end, and time is an illusion.
15. Innocence is no better than guilt.
16. There is no murder.
17. There is no reason for sexual purity, and no concept of marriage.
18. There is no reason for compassion or caring for others.
19. There is no reason for generosity or philanthropy.
20. There is no reason for kindness.
21. There is no reason for gentleness above cruelty.
22. Human joy is no greater than animal contentment.
23. There is no love beyond lust and no intimacy beyond touch.
24. Honesty is not better than lying and stealing.
25. Fidelity is not better than betrayal and adultery, and sexual taboos are myths.
26. There is no reason to protect children.
27. There is no respect for self or others.
28. There is no progress or regress, no evolution or devolution.
29. There is no truth or falsehood and no purpose of life.
30. Art and beauty are illusions.
31. There is no music above noise.
32. There is no winning or losing.

33. There is no difference between material and non-material.
34. There is only nothing.
35. Something is nothing, and nothing is something.
36. There is no meaning, and meaning is an illusion.
37. There is no justice or injustice.
38. There is no reason or knowing or wisdom.
39. There is no altruism.
40. Self-awareness and personal identity are self-delusions.
41. Other people do not exist.
42. Humans are a parasite infestation of the earth.
43. Life is useless.
44. There is no reason to say thank you.
45. There is no reason to be polite and courteous.
46. There is no reason to trust.
47. There is no reason to hope.
48. There is no reason to show honor, acknowledgement, and praise.
49. There is no reason for service.
50. There is no mercy and no forgiveness.
51. No one has a right to live.
52. The painful emotions of humans are empty and trivial.

53. Humans are only objects with complex delusions elaborated by emotions, creativity, thoughts and beliefs.
54. Nothing is important.
55. This doesn't matter.

Epilogue: But if God does exist, then   171

Bibliographic Reading List   173

About the Author   199

Introduction

The concept of a transcendent entity as the source of morality and ultimate justice is an essential foundation of rational human life and functioning. Without a transcendent authority or standard, the numerous pursuits and values of humans are merely peculiar delusions characteristic of the human species.

Those who accept the existence of God most readily are often those who have begun to observe the wonders of nature and to form a sense of closeness and caring with family and friends. In the year of his death in 1955, the universally admired scientist Albert Einstein clarified his ambivalent views: "My religion consists of a humble admiration of the illimitable superior spirit who reveals himself in the slight details we are able to perceive with our frail and feeble minds. That deeply emotional conviction of the presence of a superior reasoning power, which is revealed in the incomprehensible universe, forms my idea of God" (Calaprice, ed., *The Quotable Einstein*, pp.195-6).

It is not uncommon that around age eight to eleven or earlier, a child speaks about God, about death, and about what happens after death. The child begins to develop a degree of faith and looks for spiritual guidance.

From the age of twelve, the child may gradually begin to doubt and to question spiritual perceptions previously taken at face value as seen reflected in nature and experienced emotionally in the giving and receiving of love and caring. Doubts concerning God may then arise from various emotional and intellectual sources and challenges, such as conflict, abuse, grief, anger, sadness, as well as beliefs and pressures from teachers, peers, and the media.

In contemporary society, the philosophy of non-theism is preferred in school and university systems and supported by theories of human origin that exclude God from any explanation. Since God cannot be personally and directly observed except through the eye of faith, divine existence and spirituality fall outside the popular definition of science and are usually not considered suitable for classroom study or discussion. At most, belief in God and other philosophical ideas are considered peculiar characteristic delusions of the human species contributing something to the complexity of human evolution.

As a result, many people are growing to adulthood without belief in God. This book discusses the implications and effects of non-belief and nihilism, much of which is observed in the despair reflected in some popular music, performing arts, the decline of sexual morality, the breakdown of marriage and family, and increased violence and crime, especially against children. For evidence of this, one need only review the late societies of Eastern Europe and Russia, officially informed by atheism.

In spite of growing non-theism in society, there is a desire for altruism, love and concern for others, and respect for social order. Even those who deny God cling to values and beliefs that have only a spiritual origin, meaning, and motivation apart from mere survival instincts.

The exception to this across cultures is the phenomenon of the anti-social personality, sometimes with possible genetic origins, that may lack remorse, empathy, regard for the welfare of others, and respect for social order. Otherwise, every human being even in spite of an intellectual denial of God holds spiritual awareness, empathy, and beliefs.

Non-theism, as an intellectual conclusion rather than an emotional reaction, is based upon the notion that only the observable can be known or relied upon. The primary aim of this book is to show the impossibility of living one's life without innumerable beliefs.

Further, if one were to thoughtfully examine everything regarded as observable objective reality, one would be forced to the conclusion that objective reality does not exist in a pure absolute form without some element of subjective belief. Therefore, the foundational principle of non-theism, objective observable reality, relies upon belief.

It is beyond the scope of this volume to focus on scientific, historical, or archaeological evidence, and there is little attempt to do so. The conclusions expressed herein are based upon reason and logic.

The extensive *Bibliographic Reading List* at the end of the book presents the works of others who have thought about the existence of God. The listing is divided between atheism and theism although some listed as atheists or theists may be agnostics or skeptics and those who may believe in a metaphysical or transcendent power.

The numerous authors on both sides of the subject are presented to the reader for further study and fair consideration of this most important question.

How To Use This Book

Each numbered statement followed by a brief discussion, provides a suggestion that if there is no God then a particular conclusion follows.

The discussion for each statement presents a further elaboration including a variety of applications and implications. In most cases, a counter-point is offered for the purpose of stimulating the reader to further thought and meditation.

The reader may choose to initially review all the statements, then return to a single one each day. At the end of each discussion or elaborated conclusion, a short list of thought questions is provided which may be useful for personal reflection or for group discussion and debate.

A Word of Caution

The ideas expressed in this volume are intended to challenge and stimulate the reader's understanding of the most fundamental principles of human existence. While this can be a positive experience, some readers may feel an increase in anxiety or depression.

A value or belief shift may occur and is expected. Confusion is a normal part of the process of re-thinking one's beliefs. This may be especially the case for anyone not accustomed to considering the foundations and meaning of existence.

If the reader develops emotional discomfort, sharing one's feelings with others who are supportive and non-judgmental can be helpful. Remember that the process of searching for meaning and the associated emotions are normal and part of being human.

Meditations On Believing

1-55

1

Man is only physical and has no soul or spirit.

The idea of the human spirit or soul is the belief that each human being possesses a unique individual identity or self-awareness that continues to exist after the death of the physical body.

Whether or not there is scientific evidence for the soul is controversial and the evidence is scant at best. Yet to deny the existence of the soul, leaves humans having the same status and in the same position as that of any other matter, living or nonliving. The implications of this view are far-reaching.

It means that physical death is the end of individual existence. One might hold the view that the energy of the person changes form or is distributed to other matter and that this is a form of continuation beyond the life of the person. Yet this could be said also of any other material object.

If man has no individual soul or spirit surviving after death, there is also no moral accountability of the individual after death. The only rational approach becomes one's own self-interest and pleasure. Beyond this, life becomes a pointless exercise to end in dust and ashes.

Death occurs when the spirit or breath leaves the body. Yet the spirit is more than breath. The spirit is the unique identity of the individual, characterized by self-awareness, the act of will, moral choices and responsibility.

If there is no individual spirit, there is also no life after death and no individual accountability after death. These are spiritual ideas, the foundation of all social order and morality, and we understand these things only because God spoke to humans.

Thought Questions

1. Is the existence of the human soul that continues beyond death, only a belief, a proven scientific fact, or a subject of scientific controversy?
2. If humans have no individual identity that continues after death, what are the implications for living, for achievement, and for moral behaviour?
3. If humans have no souls, how are humans different in value and importance in relation to other animals, plants, and objects?

2

People have no greater value than other life forms.

The entire basis of social order in any culture or civilization, depends upon the belief that the human being not only possesses special value but that this value is greater than other animals, plants, insects, objects, and forces of nature.

Yet this belief is only a belief, entirely without any scientific evidence. It is an arbitrary value so profound that to reject this belief, completely undermines the concepts of society, social progress, democracy, human rights and equality.

Without this belief, humans possess no greater value than ants, slugs, and rocks, and therefore to destroy people would not be murder. Humans would be simply a particular material organization of atoms, nothing more. It would be no worse to kill people than to clear a forest or exterminate termites. Who has more right to live: humans or bacteria?

If one attempts to establish or design a hierarchy of the value of living and nonliving things, some arbitrary belief must be introduced: for example, value based on the size of the animal, or the degree of complexity of the organism, or the degree of creativity of the animal, or the kind of animal such as mammals being greater than insects, or value based on the belief that organic things are greater than inorganic things, and so on. These arbitrary beliefs lead to other problems: for example, less creative people and short people would be of less worth than tall smart people, and so on.

If humans have no greater value than other life forms, then it could be logically considered murder to kill an ant, a dog, a whale, a tree, and so on. In societies where animals are regarded as equal to humans, as in Hindu India which saves the lives of cattle while people starve, or in atheistic societies such as the former Soviet Union where humans had no souls and were expendable, the social order breaks down and people live in poverty and hopelessness.

The idea that humans should not be used and sold as pets or as beasts of burden is based not on scientific evidence but on the spiritual belief that humans possess special unique dignity and worth that sets them apart from other life forms. This is the only reason one can sell a thoroughbred horse or a goldfish but cannot sell a person.

Belief in the superior value of humans is firmly and solely based on another belief: that man was created in the image of God. With this superior value of humans comes the superior moral responsibility of humans to regard one another with the highest dignity and respect and to care for the earth. This leads directly to the protection of human rights and to the development of social order.

Thought Questions

1. Do you believe humans are superior to or more important than other species? Explain.
2. Do you believe it should be considered murder to kill an animal? Explain.
3. Describe a society in which humans possess no special value, any more than bacteria or sand.
4. Why should people not be bought and sold as one would sell a horse, a cat, or a dog?

3

There is no right and wrong, no morality, and no integrity.

The idea of right and wrong is purely a belief having no obvious scientific evidence to verify or establish it as truth. Yet there is hardly a single person not in prison or a mental institution, who would deny that right and wrong exist on some level. The rule of altruistic love, doing what is most caring in any situation, is perhaps the most widely accepted belief.

Yet if there is no God, on what basis is such a standard of conduct to be established? What is fundamentally wrong with shooting anyone in the back or taking what belongs to others without their agreement or reporting something untrue that hurts another person? These things may bring some advantage to the person who does them. Why are they wrong, not allowed, or unacceptable? If you can get away with it, why not do it?

Imagine a world with no morality. This would lead to disorder, violence, and chaos. Eventually, people would reach agreements to behave in a certain way so that individual life and property would be protected. Yet, if there were no moral standard beyond human invention, there would be no reason for the clever and powerful not to act solely in their own interest except when they wish to pacify others. Without God, there is no basis for altruistic love, only the law of the jungle.

Ultimately, any standard of right and wrong is designed by God, and this standard then is used by God to judge each person. Moreover, the venue for this judgment must finally be an existence after death.

Some hold the belief that morality is a peculiar feature of the human species and that this gives rise to social order and the rule of law for the purposes of survival of the species and the protection of young, instincts common to almost all living things. A non-theistic naturalistic worldview includes the belief that all human behaviour is natural and therefore amoral.

Yet the outcome of no real moral code and no moral accountability after death is that individuals and groups who adopt this understanding, are able to override their moral consciousness and devise schemes against the common good and the social order in order to satisfy their own desire for personal profit, power, and pleasure. This is the only rational approach if there is no God and no afterlife.

It is possible, because of the creative intelligence of humans, to overcome or subvert the rule of law.

Therefore, altruistic ideas or any concern for the common good or any regard for social order based on the rule of law, are based solely on theism and individual accountability after death. Theism is the sole foundation of moral behavior.

Thought Questions

1. What is your basis for determining right and wrong?
2. Describe a society in which there is no such thing as right and wrong?
3. Do you believe there is any origin higher than humans, for a standard of right and wrong? Explain.
4. If there is no higher spiritual origin than humans, for right and wrong, what are the implications for you and society as a whole?
5. If "morality" is naturally and genetically determined rather than a matter of individual free choice, what happens to moral responsibility?

4

Human destiny belongs to the clever and strong.

In a world without a transcendent divine moral code by which human conduct will ultimately be judged, those who are physically weak and lack survival knowledge, become the prey of the clever and strong. This is the situation now in many parts of the world and in society. Hence the need for courts, judges, and a police force. Only a society in which the people believe a divine law, can social order be maintained and kindness encouraged.

If there is no divine standard of right and wrong, human destiny is determined by those who design the most effective strategies and who have the most powerful army and weapons. This is the implication of natural selection and survival of the fittest if one takes a purely materialistic approach to existence. This was the conclusion of the atheist-informed policies of Stalin, Pol Pot, Ceauscescu, Menghistu, Kim Jong Il, and Mao Tse Tung, who have murdered more than have died in all wars.

From a non-theistic viewpoint, those who believe in love, kindness, and compassion, are in fact vulnerable, ignorant, and weak because they are limited by delusional spiritual fantasies characteristic of the primitive or progressive human animal.

In this kind of world, the definitions of virtue and nobility and the most superior examples of humanity, are those who excel in devising the greatest physical power and the most effective schemes of global conquest and control.

Thought Questions

1. Describe a society in which there is no belief in divine judgment or consequences after death for wrongs committed during one's lifetime.
2. What prevents clever and strong people from taking advantage of other people?
3. How does a moral code and human compassion for the weak affect the process of natural selection whereby the strong survive and the weak examples of the species die off?

5

The concepts of worth and value do not exist.

The concepts of worth, value, and importance are ways of organizing ideas and things according to some arbitrary criteria, a peculiar characteristic of the human animal. In fact, there exists no purely scientific basis for determining something as important.

If one says water is important for plants and animals to survive, the accurate meaning is that water is necessary or useful, not that it is important. Even to say that something is useful or necessary seems arbitrary.

A plant may need water and a child may need the plant to eat. Yet what of value is lost if a plant dies?

A child may need a parent or adult to survive. Yet what of value is lost if a child dies?

A community or nation may need some person or people to survive. Yet what of value is lost if a nation dies?

The world may need a particular nation or agreement among nations, to maintain peace. Yet what of value is lost if the world dies?

If nothing or no one outside the world values or needs the world, then the world is not important or necessary or of value, except in the peculiar thoughts of the human species that has no value.

If the world is of no transcendent value, then neither is a nation, or a people, or a child, or a plant, or anything else.

The world, its contents, and its destruction are of no importance if there is no God, and therefore nihilism or the idea that nothing has value, is the truth.

Yet there is one belief that establishes the value of all: God saw all that he had made, and it was very good.

Thought Questions

1. If there is no God, how would you explain the value or importance of life, people, love, or anything else?
2. If value is defined as something needed to survive, how would you explain the importance of survival itself?
3. What are the implications of believing that nothing has value?

6

There is no love, and love is no better than indifference.

Love is more than a feeling. It is caring for the well being of another person or people, without having any expectation of being approved or loved in return. Love is by definition performed without any ulterior motive other than the simple gratification that comes from extending love. One who gives anonymously experiences this love in a pure sense.

The opposite of love is not hate but indifference. To know someone is suffering or deprived of necessities and powerless, and yet to do nothing, is indifference or apathy. Therefore love takes action to meet the need depending on the circumstances. Love without deeds is nothing. Love is sacrificial because it is willing to suffer in order to relieve others.

What is the basis for love? Is it in any way logical to love or care for others without being loved or acknowledged in return? What purpose would it serve? The primitive instinctual need to preserve offspring is limited to the family or the social group. What is the reason for extending love to strangers or to adversaries or to those who threaten the survival of one's family?

Love in its full sense, is based solely on the fact of God's love for mankind in the gifts of life and nature and in the death of Jesus. This sacrificial divine love, once known and recognized by us, becomes the motivation for extending love to others. For this reason, after all points have been considered, love is divine and spiritual because it rests upon the fact of God's love for the world.

If there is no God, love is a foolish misguided notion. If there is no God, there is no love, for love is of God (I John 4:7).

Thought Questions

1. What is your idea of love for someone?
2. Does love mean sacrificing oneself for another? Explain.
3. If there is no God, what is the meaning and purpose of love?

7
Life is no better than death.

It is not possible to give scientific reasons to prove that life is better than death. Any special value placed on life as against death, is purely arbitrary and ultimately spiritual. The prohibition of suicide in many societies is based not on reason but on spiritual beliefs alone.

One cannot prove that humans are better than other life forms or non-life forms. Therefore, it is no more tragic to end a human life than to smash a rock.

Life has no value whatsoever because even the idea of value or worth or importance, is arbitrary and a peculiar feature of the human mind or human animal. Spiders spin webs. Ants build tunnels. Bees make honey. Humans place values on living and non-living things and even on ideas and emotions, including the idea that life is better than death.

Death has many advantages: no more physical pain, no more emotional pain, self-hatred, sadness, guilt, depression, fear, anxiety, struggles with people, loss of love, school, bullying by others, insurmountable obstacles, pressures of society, miserable work, the physical and mental decline of old age.

If there is no afterlife, there is no motivation to endure unbearable pain and suffering. The suffering of Jesus and his resurrection is our example and hope when we face suffering and death. Those born again by God, are able not only to endure great pain but can also feel a certain honour and oneness with Him who suffered more than anyone and on our behalf.

Without this view of things, life has no real point other than the shallow pursuits of food, shelter, and family life true as well of any animal species. The belief that life is better than death is based solely on the idea that the human spirit is from God and is the very object of his great love.

God alone gives our lives ultimate purpose: to love and serve God and to love our fellow humans as much as we love ourselves and knowing that God loved all people so much that he gave his Son to bear all of their offenses.

Thought Questions

1. Do you believe life is better than death? Explain.
2. If there is no God, how is life better than and different than death?
3. Who defines what life is and what death is? Explain.
4. How are life and death different other than the physical signs?

8

There is no difference between life and non-life.

Even that which is regarded as non-life, has mass and energy. The atoms comprising all matter including humans have a nucleus, electrons, protons, and neutrons, and a process so dynamic that an explosion can be produced so powerful that a relatively small number of atoms have the potential to destroy all of mankind. Popular science maintains that atoms are not alive.

The commonly accepted scientific definition of life contains a spiritual belief. Life is defined as something that reproduces or has a metabolic process. This definition states that life is demonstrated in functions such as metabolism, growth, reproduction, and response to stimuli or adaptations to the environment generated from within the organism.

Yet if one looks at the "non-living" parts of the earth, sun, and universe one can observe processes, which fit this definition. One can observe the birth of planets, suns, solar systems, and galaxies. There is metabolism on a massive scale of matter, heat, energy, and gravitational fields, within suns, galaxies, and black holes. There is also observable growth and response to stimuli and adaptation to the environment within and among suns, planets, and galaxies.

Is there life in the universe other than earth? If we simply expand the definition of life to include the entire universe, the concept of death becomes void since dynamic processes characterize everything.

The popular scientific definition of life is in reality a purely spiritual belief based on the early account that God breathed into man's nostrils the breath of life and man became a living soul, that life is in the blood, and that living things would be "fruitful and multiply" (reproduction), and that God gives to everything life and breath. When the metabolism of oxygen or breath of life ceases, death follows for any living thing. Death occurs when the spirit leaves the body.

This is true only because God declares it to be so. Otherwise, if there is no God, we can expand the definition of life and death to include whatever we wish. In this way, even popular science without intending, acknowledges God through adherence to one of the most fundamental concepts: the distinction between life and death.

Thought Questions

1. How does human death relate to the idea of a human soul?
2. How does the scientific definition of life apply to non-living things?
3. What ideas about death depend upon the existence of God?

9

There is no hope beyond death, and death is the end.

Life without hope is the definition of despair. Non-theism addresses only what is observed. Although attempts are made to observe the soul through scientific approaches or to document reports of life after death through near-death experiences, these areas of study are controversial and the evidence being presented is of questionable scientific validity.

Yet reason would dictate that there must be life after death because to deny any existence after death, means that death is the end of the individual. If death is the end of the individual, then any effort during life is without value. Morality becomes meaningless and suicide becomes a reasonable way to escape any pain and discomfort.

Pleasure becomes the central goal of life, and the lives of other people become means to this end. Yet if death is the end, pleasure being transient seems futile and serves only to tease and frustrate the psyche.

If death is all there is, human bonds and affection are cruel and shallow fantasies enticing one toward the bitter end of grief. If death is the end of the individual, one might argue that some kind of hope can be established in the belief that striving for progress, arbitrarily defined, contributes to evolutionary improvements in the species as a whole.

This belief requires arbitrary definitions of progress, evolution, and improvement. Non-theism contains fundamental assumptions behind these arbitrary definitions, requiring still further arbitrary definitions and assumptions.

For example, progress is defined as moving toward increased complexity or functional organization. So the terms complexity, functional, and organization require some arbitrary definition.

Complexity may refer to having increased numbers of observable interactive parts. This then requires a definition of that which qualifies as a single number and what constitutes interaction. A single number then may be defined as anything observable or identifiable such as parts of an atom or a unit or particle of light (photon).

The term "observable" requires definition, excluding or including subjective experiences such as thoughts, logical structures and reasons, ideas, and emotions. The idea of interaction requires an arbitrary definition to distinguish it from that which is not interactive. A reasonable argument could be presented for the view that everything is interactive which then undermines the entire notion of complexity since complexity depends upon the interactivity of a group of parts.

What constitutes a group and then a part of a group? The difficulties of definition are endless and require endless definitions based on endless assumptions.

If there is a God, there is a beginning based on a single belief: In the beginning, God... (Genesis 1:1). There is a foundation of knowledge: God who says: I am that I am, (Exodus 3:14), the beginning and the end (Revelation 1:8).

If there is no God, tyranny and genocide are important because they serve the purpose of increasing and exercising the strength or ability of an individual, a society, or a species to overcome adversity, which then requires an arbitrary definition.

Without the challenges of tyranny and genocide, the species becomes weak and therefore vulnerable to extinction, not that this is undesirable depending upon one's definition of what is desirable.

On this reasoning, the tyrant is a hero of the continuing struggle of evolution in the survival of the strongest. But evolution toward what? Who defines the ideal species and the goal of evolution, if there is a goal?

Is the possible goal not to become extinct and to give way to something new? Or is the goal to dominate? Or is it to become intangible? Or to become energy? The goal must be arbitrary, based on some belief.

If there is no God, there is no goal. Therefore, the goal of human existence is based on a single belief: Divine revelation tells us to fear God and keep his teachings, for this is the whole purpose of mankind (Ecclesiastes 12:13).

Scientists often report that the death of the earth will occur with changes in the heat of the sun. Some say the sun will become what is termed a "red giant" preceding the incineration of earth.

If there is nothing beyond the death of the earth, what is the value of anyone living a moral or compassionate life? What is the value of trying to accomplish anything? All is in vain, if there is no God and nothing beyond this life for the individual.

If human choices end in the grave and have no eternal effect, then human endeavour in all its elaborate glory is only a grand illusion. Consider all the great cities, all the inventions and technology, all the art and literature, all the murder, war and genocide, with all the victory and defeat in the name of truth, noble virtues and rights of men. They are all fantasies of the human species. Tulips are as worthy as humans and perhaps superior for their use of life unwasted on such delusions and vain efforts.

Indeed, as the apostle Paul says, If we only hope in Christ in this life, we are the most hopeless of all people (1 Corinthians 15:19).

Thought Questions

1. If there is no individual existence after death, what is the purpose of life?
2. If there is no individual existence after death, how are humans different than animals or trees in this regard?
3. If there is no individual existence after death, what are the implications for personal behaviour?

10

There is no purpose or design in the universe.

If there is no God, there is no purpose or explanation for the universe because the purpose requires a belief rather than scientific proof. Without God, the universe simply exists although existence itself requires an element of belief that there is a difference between existence and non-existence.

All parts of the universe and the earth appear to have a design. Whether or not evolution is true, is irrelevant to the fact that order and design are characteristics of all things observable as well as the inner life or psyche of plants and animals.

Consider the astonishing design and creativity of tangible things: the delicate balance of the earth's ecosystem, temperature, water, air, soil, the changing seasons and climactic regions, the organization of an atom and of a single cell, photosynthesis, locomotion and reproduction of plants and animals, the fields of gravity on earth and in space, galaxies, solar systems, the instinctual behavior of species of animals, the intricate and complex design of living things from plants and single-celled organisms such as paramecium to humans with their creative ability. The complex technology of non-human creativity in the "natural process" of the universe far exceeds anything humans have designed with all of their determination, moral sense, self-awareness, and intelligence.

Is there something or some force or energy behind this order and complex design? Does it exist eternally? The idea of a non-living matter over any length of time organizing itself to grow a brain, set up a university, then build a rocket to the moon is completely irrational, and this is the elephant in the evolution living room. The idea of an eternal transcendent intelligence behind all natural processes, is the only logical conclusion also because a closed-system universe requires the contribution of information to produce increasing complexity.

Contained within the observable universe, are human beings who have the unusual ability to exercise choice and volition, to be self-aware and creative, and possessing moral sense and intelligence. These human attributes and abilities may be the key to understanding the source of the dynamic natural processes observed throughout the universe.

Man-made things can be observed and distinguished as having order and design, a reflection of what is seen in the universe that is not man-made but which nonetheless has order and design. Human intelligence has produced technology and design. Therefore it is reasonable to conclude that the advanced non-human technology and design observed in the universe is the product of advanced non-human intelligence.

The creative intelligence of humans made in God's image, is therefore a reflection of the creative intelligence of the universe. This creative intelligence seen in the order and design of the universe must also contain self-awareness because it is experienced as a characteristic of human beings who are creative but to an extent far inferior to that seen in the universe.

God can be understood as greater than the whole, the sum of the parts of the universe. Since the universe includes self-awareness and creativity, God who is greater than the whole, also contains these characteristics of creativity and self-awareness. Therefore, God "the Creator" is the source and origin of the universe in whom all things exist. The invisible attributes of God, including his power and divine attributes are clearly observable, being understood through what has been made (Romans 1:20).

Thought Questions

1. Are there any examples of the absence of "design" in the universe?
2. Is the presence of design throughout the universe, caused by accidental chance or by deliberate intention?
3. If humans are able to engage in creative design because of their intelligence, is it reasonable to conclude that the advanced non-human complex design observed throughout the universe is also the result of some kind of advanced non-human intelligence?
4. What do you believe is the purpose of the universe?

11

Peace is not better than war.

Peace is perhaps a value for those who want to live without fear, but for others, peace is boring, and war is interesting and exciting. In the fifth century C.E., Augustine worked out arbitrary conditions of a justifiable war and said war is just if it is an act of self-defense. Those who believe in a just war theory, still believe peace is desirable. Others, who believe in an absolute ethic of non-resistance, hold that all use of force against evil is wrong.

Yet all of these views are based upon spiritual values. If there is no God, neither peace nor war can be demonstrated to be preferable. It may be argued from a non-theist view that war challenges the species to develop survival skills and helps the process of natural selection through survival of the fittest.

Besides this, if there is no God, life has no meaning anyway, so to live or die, or to kill or be killed, makes no difference. Why live in peace? Why not make power, control, and violence the purpose of your life? It's as valid as any other purpose.

The only reason to believe that peace is best, is because there is a God who "so loved the world" who says, "Love your enemies" and "Love your neighbor" and "Blessed are the peacemakers." Only God gives worthwhile meaning, value, and direction to our lives.

Thought Questions

1. What are the useful purposes of war?
2. How can one establish that war contributes to natural selection?
3. Assuming there is no God, why would peace be undesirable?
4. Is the value of peace a personal belief or a scientific fact?

12

Humans are not responsible for the care of the earth.

It is nearly impossible to find anyone who denies that humans are responsible for the care and keeping of the earth. No one says whales are responsible for the earth and its resources, or that monkeys are responsible, or apes, or dolphins, or any other creature.

The very concept of responsibility by definition, includes moral obligation. If one does not fulfill one's duty or responsibility, the result is that one is irresponsible and has failed or shirked, which are moral terms. Only humans are viewed in this way.

If there is no God, then there are no consequences for polluting the air, water, and soil, or for causing entire species to become extinct. If humans cause these things to occur, from a non-theist point of view, it is simply part of the amoral course of nature until perhaps humans become extinct giving way to other species. In other words, it's not a bad thing, just something that happens.

Non-theistic teaching in the educational system, is leaving out an essential spiritual foundation of the relationship between humans and nature. The idea that humans are responsible for the earth, is based solely on a spiritual belief, that God who rules the universe, made mankind in his own image and designed humans to rule over animals and over all the earth (Genesis 1:26). This responsibility is not believed to belong to any other species.

Thought Questions

1. Are humans more responsible than elephants, for taking care of the earth's environment? Why or why not?
2. Is it important for the earth and it's species to survive? Why or why not?
3. Is human responsibility for taking care of the earth a spiritual belief? Why or why not?

13

Freedom is not better than slavery.

Philosophers who founded modern democracy declared the inalienable rights of life, liberty, and the pursuit of happiness and affirm that every human being is created equal and endowed with these rights by the Creator. Yet this is certainly an arbitrary set of spiritual beliefs having no scientific foundation.

If there is no God, it may be said with equal validity that people have a variety of degrees of worth and that the weak are best suited to serve the clever and strong. It can be affirmed that no inherent human rights exist, and that rather than rights to be observed and protected, it is the law of natural selection and survival of the fittest which prevail, not by virtue of any court or social order but by means of power and wit.

If one is free to kill, one is also able to be killed by another who has the same freedom. Altruism, or concern for the welfare of others, is based on the desire for self-preservation but assumes that the concern for others and the defense of others' rights, will be reciprocated. This motive of self-preservation is not true altruism.

This is an optimistic view of human nature and assumes others hold the same philosophy. History, however, has proven otherwise. One need only look to capitalism, Nazism, ethnic cleansing, nationalism, fascism, communism, totalitarianism, slavery, and other human organized efforts and movements. These realities demonstrate that altruism is an ideal based upon a spiritual belief leading to democracy.

The survival instinct, derived from biological evolution, is far too self-centered to extend to the development of democracy. Rather, democratic principles such as the definition and protection of human rights, must rely upon purely spiritual values of equal human worth which in turn relies on the belief that each human is a reflection of God.

Thought Questions

1. What are the benefits of slavery?
2. If there is no God, would not slavery serve the purpose of natural selection?
3. Who has decided that everyone is created equal and deserves freedom?

14

There is no beginning and no end, and time is an illusion.

The idea of time is an abstract human idea, a belief, and not a scientific fact. Yet time is so basic to our existence that without such a belief, humans would not be able to organize their lives. Time is the basis of all human accomplishment, human will and choice. Non-human life has no need for time because their lives are governed not by their choice but by instinct and "natural law".

Scientific fact is defined fundamentally by that which is observed. Time by its passing nature, cannot be observed. The past cannot be observed. Therefore the past does not exist. The future cannot be observed. Therefore the future does not exist. The present cannot be observed because it is always moving into the past.

The present at best is only a theoretical concept. Since scientific proof or fact depends upon three repeated observations, the present cannot be proven even by a second observation. Therefore, the present does not exist.

Time is based on the setting and rising sun, phases of the moon, the changing seasons, and the observation of the birth, growth, and death of plants, animals, and people. Yet these arbitrary determinations of time find their reflection in spiritual history that in the beginning God created the heavens and the earth (Genesis 1:1).

The seven-day week comes from the seven days of creation described originally in the book of Genesis, lost knowledge taken for granted by modern society. From this, the concept of time proceeds to order the workdays of technocrats and nomads.

Without these markers for time, one would be just as correct to say that there is no beginning and no end to anything: to the universe to the earth, or to human life. In other words, it could be said that life neither begins nor ends but merely is or is not. Now you see it, now you don't. There is no birth as a beginning, only as a continuation, and no death as an end, only as a transformation into other matter and energy.

Imagine being on another planet where the suns and or moons move differently than on earth. Suddenly the seasons disappear, and what happens to minutes and hours? Weeks? Months? Years? These are all functions of time on earth.

At best then, we can only speak of earth time, and so time is founded upon the spiritual history of earth and only useful for human purposes. Other species have no awareness of time and no need to be consciously aware of time.

Why do humans need time? While other species are slaves to daily and seasonal cycles, humans approach time consciously with the ability and responsibility to make choices, to organize, to work, and to rest, all reflections of God who created in six days and rested on the seventh.

Time is a human construct attached to physical human existence and creativity. If there is no God, the human sense of awareness, consciousness, and sense of time are delusions peculiar to the human animal.

If science is based upon what is observed, events of the past and of passing moments, are matters of faith as the past cannot be observed directly in the present but must rely upon corroborative evidence. Similarly, the existence of the future is a matter of speculation more than of faith, for there is no evidence to support the future.

There is no beginning and no end, no passing, no past, no present, and no future for which animals prepare by instinct. These ideas of time are all functions of the human need to reflect, to choose, to plan, and to create, which only find reality in the spiritual belief that God, who transcends time, made the beginning and made man in God's image.

Time is a matter of faith declared by the first words of scripture that records the commencement of time: In the beginning God.....

Thought Questions

1. How could you make the case that time is not an observable scientific fact?
2. Why is time a belief peculiar to humans?
3. Why is time important to humans more than to other beings?

15

Innocence is no better than guilt.

In fact, if there is no God, the concepts of guilt and innocence have no meaning beyond the social order which itself is founded upon a theistic-based belief in the welfare of society or the common good.

The emotion of guilt is a peculiar feature of the human personality calling attention to the sense that one has done something wrong or failed to do something right. Even if there were no human laws against murder, for example, a normal human would feel guilt about killing another human. This may indicate a spiritual reality, without scientific proof or necessity that sets human beings apart from other animals.

If there is no God, this sense of guilt is a baseless delusional feature of humans. Guilt prevents humans from engaging in selfish acts, those that may serve the individual but not the society. Guilt is based only upon a belief in a divine standard of conduct and a concern for the welfare of others, which have no foundation if there is no God.

Non-theism proposes that behavior is only a matter of practicality, what works or does not work, to achieve a desired purpose such as civil order and progress, arbitrarily defined. The purpose of order and progress is to provide an environment for evolution.

The purpose of evolution is an advanced species that has no definition, other than perhaps that it is successful, defined as still existing perhaps in large numbers that dominate or intimidate other species. However, this would occur without civil order, and there is no basis in non-theism to postulate that one species ought to survive based on any particular measure of importance.

The conclusion is that social concern based only on practicality, is empty because it calls upon the individual to value the future of the human species beyond one's own existence, a future that is directed by natural processes regardless of the efforts of a single human.

Social concern, right and wrong, guilt and innocence, are spiritual ideas based upon both a belief in the value of others and in individual accountability to God after death.

Thought Questions

1. Why are the ideas of guilt and innocence only human beliefs rather than scientific facts?
2. Describe a society in which there is no such thing as guilt and innocence.

3. If there is no God, how can guilt and innocence be important?

16

There is no murder.

Murder is an assumed idea of human society and without any scientific foundation. Animal species other than man have no concept of murder. They kill one another as a matter of survival without regard for any right to life. Humans kill other species, both plants and animals, for food. Millions of other species, such as viruses and bacteria, are eliminated because of their threat to humans, yet it is not considered murder.

The idea of murder assumes a number of spiritual beliefs. First, the right of a human being to live. Second, the value of human life compared to other life forms. Third, the idea of justice or the deserved punishment or consequences for murder. Fourth, the idea of what is serious, an offense, right and wrong behavior, a standard of morality.

To murder a human being is considered to be the most serious of all offenses, deserving the death of the one who commits a murder. It is not considered murder to kill an ant or a mosquito unless it is so defined by the spiritual beliefs of a culture. Yet few versions of atheism short of Stalin's example, would assert that murder extends to other species or that taking a human life against his will is not murder.

There is an extraordinary and arbitrary value placed upon human life, yet without explanation. Ultimately, the only explanation for the idea of murder as a foundation of human social order, is that humans are a reflection of the divine, or that they have a soul, or that the divine has placed superior value upon humans and instructed humans to observe this value.

There is no reason to believe scientifically that other life forms or even what is considered non-life, are devoid of an eternal soul or spirit.

Thought Questions

1. If there is no God, is murder wrong?
2. Why is it not murder to kill an ant?
3. What makes humans so special that makes killing a human more serious than killing a mosquito?

17

There is no reason for sexual purity, and no concept of marriage.

Sexual practice is only a matter of personal pleasure, and therefore the moral social taboos intended to protect the gene pool as in the case of incest for example, are without foundation when safe sex is observed. All sexual boundaries and prohibitions are based upon spiritual beliefs.

Marriage as a union between one man and one woman is an arbitrary belief. In the absence of divine law, marriage could be defined as a union of three or more persons, of any gender combination, and of any biological relationship. In India a man married his dog.

The sexual "age of consent" is arbitrary and could be easily changed to include anyone of any age or species who feels "comfortable" in a sexual relationship. Marriage could be defined as a temporary or momentary state, severable by either party for any reason.

The only foundation for marriage as a union between one man and one woman having a mutual commitment for a lifetime, is found in ancient words stating that a man will leave his father and his mother, and be joined to his wife, and they will then be one (Genesis 2:24).

Thought Questions

1. If there is no God, what are the implications for sexual behaviour?
2. What sexual behaviours appear to have no physically harmful affects?
3. Why are sexual values really human beliefs without scientific validity?

18

There is no reason for compassion or caring for others.

Weak members of society should be allowed to die because they are not fit to survive. This is the reasonable conclusion of non-theistic evolution.

Some have reasoned that compassion is part of the highly evolved nature of human beings that brings the human species collectively to a higher level. The point against this, is that compassion is either an individual choice or it is predetermined by our genetic code. An example is the evidence supporting a hereditary origin for the anti-social personality, who has little or no capacity for empathy for the suffering of others.

On the surface, this would seem to indicate that empathy or compassion is part of the genetic code for humans. However, the genetic factor is about *capacity* for compassion, meaning it is a choice for those humans who do not lack the genetic capacity for compassion as in the case of some anti-social personalities.

If the capacity for compassion arises from the genetic ability to empathize with the pain of others, then with the ability comes the choice to show compassion or not. If one believes intellectually that only the fittest should survive, as non-theistic evolution implies, then there is a moral obligation to ignore the suffering of others.

The other counterpoint is that one's own desire to survive in life- threatening situations, gives rise to one's desire to care for others in the hope that others will reciprocate. Therefore, the higher "value" of compassion for others is based upon the lower survival instinct.

The whole idea of instinct in humans is based on the belief that humans ultimately have no truly free choice to live or die, to kill, to steal, but are driven to "moral" behaviour by instinct, except for the genetically defective anti-social personality.

The difficulty with this reasoning is that genetics determines the capacity, rather than the compulsion or necessity, of "moral" behaviour.

Thought Questions

1. What are the reasons for showing compassion and caring for others?
2. Why is it not wiser to be selfish?

3. How does one establish the value and worth of others deserving of compassion?

19

There is no reason for generosity or philanthropy.

The rationale behind contributing to alleviate the suffering of the weak is completely dependent upon the belief that the weak individuals of the human species possess worth. All social programs and private or non-profit charitable organizations exist because of the prevalent belief that it is somehow good or noble or virtuous to help people who are disadvantaged in some way.

An alternative belief is to view the weak as a burden on humanity. Think of the resources that could be diverted from charity and directed toward technological advances. This assumes however, that technological advances are somehow good or noble and a suitable object of generosity.

If a society does not care for the poor, the poor will rise up in rebellion to destroy or change the governing power. Therefore it is in the self-interest of any government to provide a social safety net. This becomes a question of survival of the state, not a matter of altruistic feeling for those who suffer.

Yet in a truly non-theistic state, the poor are seen only as a burden on society and a threat to the state. The infamous atheist Joseph Stalin of the former Soviet Union, took this view and destroyed many of the poor as well as any perceived enemies to a total of 30,000,000 lives by some estimates.

All social programs that proceed from democracies are based upon the spiritual altruistic beliefs of the people. The scientific atheism of communism, could not inspire the commitment of the people to work because a system devoid of a spiritual centre has no heart and no reason for existence.

There is no objective scientific support for the practice of contributing to life at all, let alone human life or its advancement. This would assume the superior importance of any form of life or of human life, but on what grounds? The answer is that only a spiritual belief can support such behaviour.

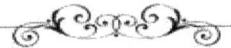

Thought Questions

1. How can you make the case that human generosity is based on a delusion?
2. If there is no God, how is it considered immoral to help the poor?
3. Why is helping the poor and sick, based on a purely spiritual belief?

20

There is no reason for kindness.

Kindness is the act or attitude of a positive sense of giving or of well-wishing toward others. It is characterized by sincerity and genuineness conveyed by voice tone and facial expression through a smile. It is sensitivity and consideration for the needs of others, an understanding and empathy for the pain of others, and taking action based on a desire to help others. Sometimes kindness requires doing for others what they need although they may not desire it, because it is known to be in their best interest.

Why would someone want to be kind if there is no reward or recognition, but only the satisfaction gained in lending aid? This self-sacrificing act has no basis in self-preservation or the survival instinct, because it is extended purely from the apparent irrational motive to find satisfaction in giving.

Kindness motivated purely by self-survival, because one wants others to be kind to oneself, is one possible way of life. Yet with the same motivation, one might commit treachery and murder. Virtues motivated by self-survival are therefore not virtues for they lack any sincere caring for others.

Why would anyone find satisfaction in acts of kindness as an end in itself with no selfish motive? Kindness is illogical without a spiritual belief that raises kindness to the highest value, an attribute of God and a result of union with the divine. If there is no God, there is no true kindness.

Thought Questions

1. Without God, what is the rationale for kindness?
2. How can kindness be selfless or selfish?
3. How is true kindness only possible by knowing God?

21

There is no reason for gentleness above cruelty.

Gentleness is based upon a value for reducing conflict, respecting the worth of others, and desiring to ameliorate the physical or emotional pain of others. Cruelty and rudeness are regarded as wrong behaviour because they devalue others.

Cruelty and torture are practiced by governments as ways of obtaining information, yet they are condemned by humanitarian organizations. Cruelty toward animals is monitored and condemned by the Society for the Prevention of Cruelty to Animals on the belief that it is wrong.

Terrorists are condemned because of their practices, which kill and maim the innocent as ways of putting pressure on governments to submit to certain political aims. There are those who delight in cruelty and torture. History is filled with those who find fulfillment in such acts, from schoolyard bullies and abusive parents to Hitler and his friends. Cruelty can provide a sense of addictive power needing to be fed.

Other human beings are seen as having little value, and their feelings are nonexistent or unimportant. Other people are means to the end of feeling better, stronger, and more important. The suffering, crying, and pain of the victims show their weakness, and their deserved purpose is to serve as entertainment for the strong.

Thought Questions

1. If there is no God, what is the harm of sadism?
2. Why does the wrong of cruelty require a belief in the worth of human beings?
3. Why is gentleness a sign of weakness based on a delusion?

22

Human joy is no greater than animal contentment.

An animal is in a relaxed state of activity when it is fed and rested and when its offspring are safe. Human joy is believed to have some superior and even spiritual quality compared to other animal species.

Human happiness comes from many sources beyond the satisfaction of basic needs: harmony and closeness in relationships, meaning and purpose in life, accomplishment, and resolution of grief, for example. These elements spring from choice, which is the basis of all mental health in humans; whereas animals cannot choose to grieve, resolve conflict, or create their direction in life.

Humans are the masters of their destiny. It is the sense of personal power and self-determination that brings fulfillment, and that animals cannot enjoy. Humans feel joy derived from love for others, while animals possess only an instinctual loyalty to the pack and respond to the stimulation of food.

If there is no God, there is no reason for joy and happiness. These emotions reach no deeper and possess no greater significance than the moment or at most the period of a single human life. These emotions are believed to be characteristic of all life forms when needs are met and in humans are associated with other pleasures or psychological needs such as recognition, greeting a loved one, when justice is done.

Human joy is on several levels beginning with meeting basic physical needs for food and shelter, then extending to emotional needs as in relationships with other humans, then the sense of self-actualization through exercising one's potential through creative choice, and lastly through achieving a sense of meaning and purpose or self-realization.

If there is no God, the range of joy and happiness becomes limited. The satisfaction of basic physical needs, shared among all animals, is limited to warmth and a full stomach. Human joy in basic needs goes beyond other animals, if it recognizes and celebrates the Giver of all good things.

Without the spiritual element to define the meaning of life and the destiny of the soul, emotional needs and human relationships become shallow, and the value of one's potential and of finding purpose in life is diminished.

In God, one finds fulfillment and sustenance for the body and soul because in God we live and move and have our existence (Acts 17:28).

Thought Questions

1. Explain why human joy is different than animal contentment.
2. If humans have no soul, what is their joy based on?
3. What gives depth and meaning to human joy?

23

There is no love beyond lust and no intimacy beyond touch.

Humans have found the understanding of human love to be so attractive and powerful yet elusive, that practitioners of all art forms have tried to express and define it. Something all agree upon is that love is more than hormonal desire or mere physical attraction. The effort to define love compels one to use spiritual words.

Love can only be expressed in spiritual terms. It has been said that love is a sharing or merging of two hearts. Love reaches into the soul. Love cherishes another to the point of seeking to possess, control, even destroy, or to let go and die from starvation or suicide.

The non-spiritual scientific explanation is that love is merely the natural coupling process that characterizes the human animal. This relegates art and poetry to an animal expression similar to the mating rituals of birds, insects, and other animals.

What is human intimacy or closeness? It is the joining of two hearts, the sharing of two lives, two dreams, two joys, and two hurts. Intimacy is known through emotions of the one felt by the other. Yet this goes deeper than the tangible or the observable.

Human intimacy involves two people who are sensitive to the emotions and needs of the other. The two individuals are open and transparent with their thoughts and emotions, springing from a deep desire for the well being of the other through all difficulties.

This closeness is based upon shared values, beliefs, hopes and dreams while supporting the unique creative abilities and differences in perspective and needs. Understood and defined as such, within the fulfillment of altruism essential to intimacy, the human relationship is spiritual, consisting of abstract intangibles that rely entirely upon subjective experience and belief.

If there is no God, intimacy is reduced to a biological function for physical stimulation or reproduction of the species. There is no foundation for sensitivity or for sincere and selfless devotion. There is no basis for monogamous loyalty.

In the absence of spirituality, the human relationship is used for one's own purposes regardless of the interests of the other. Mutuality is replaced by self-interest, and loyal devotion is replaced by uncertainty, distrust, conflict, and withdrawal. Intimacy is lost in loneliness.

Only within the spirituality of intimacy can one find contentment in mutual acceptance, belonging, togetherness, and faithfulness for strength to endure the challenges of life.

Thought Questions

1. What are the spiritual aspects of love and intimacy?
2. If love is only about basic instincts, what are the implications?
3. If there is no God, how can selfless devotion exist?

24

Honesty is not better than lying and stealing.

Honesty is not a value shared by all societies. In some Eastern subcultures there is a saying: Any fool can tell the truth, but it requires a man of some sense to lie well. Deepak Chopra recently said spontaneity is better than morality which he says is "overrated." The individual or society espousing this idea, suffers abject poverty and misery above others who fear God.

Honesty requires some sense of caring for others and for society. One may lie as a protection from punishment or from a feared consequence, and this is believed to be excusable by many unless one lies to hide an offense against society requiring restitution or deserving of punishment. To lie for personal profit or pleasure, is commonly regarded as anti-social or against society.

If there is no God, the virtue of honesty whose aim is justice loses its foundation. This is the struggle of every successful society, a collection of individuals trying to live together. Without belief in a higher power, the motivation to tell the truth may come from a desire to cooperate or to avoid legal consequences.

Yet if there is no accountability higher than human courts and authorities, the individual will believe and may indeed be clever enough to lie on his tax return, steal a steak, cheat on his wife, steal from his employer, cheat on an exam, lie to investors and divert their funds, and lie to the voting public.

There was a young man who decided there is no God and no accountability after death. He felt a new freedom from rules. He thought, "Since there is no God and no judgment after I die, I will do whatever benefits me. After all, the purpose of life is my own self-interest, and that end justifies any means." He reasoned that no means to his pleasure require justification because the concepts of fair and right and compassion no longer exist.

As the young man grew, he plagiarized in college, became promiscuous, impregnated many women, demanded abortions, and became wealthy by operating a prostitution network, money lending and extortion. He has thought it expedient to eliminate rivals and sometimes to frighten others who refuse his demands. He travels widely and owns many properties and luxury vehicles. He married a woman to look after him and has had many affairs.

He decided, and logically so, that if there is no God and no divine judgment, there is no standard of conduct. If one is clever enough, one can elude civil authorities and live to an old age.

Thought Questions

1. Without God, what is wrong with lying and stealing?
2. Any fool can tell the truth, but it requires a man of some sense to lie well. Do you agree?
3. If you can advance yourself by lying and stealing, is it not an obligation or practical necessity to do so?

25

Fidelity is not better than betrayal and adultery, and sexual taboos are myths.

Sexual boundaries are based upon spiritual beliefs about what is considered moral and immoral. Even the rules that anything is acceptable as long as there is no physical harm or as long as there is mutual consent, break down since these beliefs are predicated on the most basic belief that humans have value above other creatures. If you can harm, kill, and eat or otherwise exploit an animal without their consent, why not a human, if humans have no greater value?

If there is no God, then sexual behaviour is only a matter of personal choice, with no spiritual or real consequences. Group sex is an option as well as sex in public. Then add sex with children and minors, incest between parents and children, or between siblings. Homosexual preference is a possibility, and also sex with animals and corpses. Bestiality is legal in the most secular societies of Germany, Norway, Sweden, Denmark, and Belgium. Sex with anyone or anything at anytime are acceptable, perhaps with protection or with consent or not, depending upon whether or not it is considered harmful or just a "hang-up" of the non-consenting party.

As reprehensible as these sexual behaviours may be to theists and non-theists alike, sexual boundaries, morality, and fidelity are based only on beliefs and directions given by God regarding sexuality, who said, You must not commit adultery (Exodus 20:14).

The social effects of non-theism and of the diversity of beliefs regarding sexuality are the loss of commitment and cohesion of the family. With the loss of cohesion, comes the alienation of individuals who are unable to maintain lasting healthy trusting relationships. This results in depression and in many cases addiction.

Thought Questions

1. Describe a society in which there are no sexual standards.
2. Why be faithful to a spouse who becomes sick or poor?
3. If there is no God, what's wrong with group sex or sex with animals?

26

There is no reason to protect children.

Some species eat their young. Humans may have reason to do the same with equal validity if there is no God. The abuse and exploitation of children is believed to be unacceptable in "modern" Western societies. In other societies, children may be made to work long hours in exchange for simple nourishment. They may be placed into prostitution or sent to fight a war or forced into child marriage.

Whether inside or outside the womb, children become expendable when they cost too much to feed or simply place a hardship on the parent. Sometimes children contribute little or nothing to the household income but are rather a drain. If a cat or other animal eats or kills its young, there is no thought of destroying the parent, and it should be no different for humans if there is no God.

The children of the poor in any society, including third world countries, should be allowed to starve to death. They only add numbers to the massive underclass, which contributes nothing to the evolutionary advancement of the human race.

Children in poverty should be made to work. As cheap labour, they would help reduce the cost of production. If they die from exhaustion or malnutrition, this is a reasonable fate for weak examples of the species.

In contrast, God places the highest value on children by sayng, unless one becomes like a child, one cannot enter the kingdom of God (Matthew 18:3).

Thought Questions

1. Do children have value if they do not work?
2. Is it important to save starving children in poor countries?
3. If there is no God, how can a child's life be said to have value especially if his survival is not required to continue the species?

27

There is no respect for self or others.

The idea of respect refers to regarding a person as having value or importance. Respect is conveyed in specific actions such as speaking without judgmental terms, name-calling, and demeaning language. It includes courtesy, politeness, and consideration for other's needs and desires. To give respect means also to give attention to the thoughts and emotions of another and to express empathy, feeling with the pain of the other.

One respects or values children by giving them nurturing, sustenance, guidance, protection, and letting go when they are old enough to be in their own. One respects or values a spouse by listening, being affectionate, conciliatory, and thoughtful.

One respects or values parents by considering their guidance, visiting them in senior years, and finding one's own way in life rather than burdening them. One respects or values the law by rendering obedience.

One respects or values oneself by being supportive of self, honest with self, taking care of one's emotions and body, and achieving one's full potential. One respects and values other people by attending to those in need and showing regard without distinction.

One respects or values God by following his teaching, prayer and worship, and respecting and valuing those mentioned above. If there is no God, the respect and value due to God finds no expression or reflection in one's relationship to others. With the foundation lost, there is nothing on which to build.

Thought Questions

1. If respect depends upon the value and importance of something or someone, how does one determine value?
2. If there is no God, how can anything have value?
3. How is the concept of value a matter of spirituality?

28

There is no progress or regress,

no evolution or devolution.

The definitions of progress, or civilized, or modern, and their opposites: regress, uncivilized, and primitive, are based upon arbitrary beliefs with assumptions about advancement, improvement, social values, technical knowledge, and artistic design, as examples.

Evolution contains the fundamental and arbitrary belief that increased interdependent cells and organisms are more evolved than single-celled organisms and that organic forms are more evolved than chemical forms. There is also an associated concept of value related to "complexity" whereby humans are more complex than other animals, large animals than small animals, animals than plants, plants than single-celled organisms, organic matter than non-organic matter, and so on.

There are no objective scientific criteria for the definition of a species as more highly evolved than another. One could easily argue that species of tiny water bears are the most highly evolved because they live everywhere on earth and in every environment. Their existence has been reported in hot springs, on top of the Himalayas, under five meters of solid ice and in deep ocean sediments.

However, humans may in fact constitute devolution or regression if they contribute to the extinction of other species or of the planet. According to scientific findings, other species have existed longer than humans, and on this basis may be considered more evolved because they are more adaptive or resilient than humans.

Evolution is based entirely upon a belief in the superiority of one species over another. The creativity of humans, their propensity for building cities, armies, universities, computers, and space ships, is evidence of their highly evolved and deserved status, assigned by themselves. These abilities are identified by humans to define the meaning of advancement and civilization thus declaring their superiority over other species.

A further implication of the lack of objective scientific criteria for evolution is that science apart from faith in God, has no way of establishing a moral code defining murder as the killing of humans rather than worms. In the absence of belief in God that says humans are made in God's image, there is no solid foundation for affirming the superior status of humans over other species or objects.

Thought Questions

1. By what standard is evolution defined?
2. Make the case that the human species is a parasite infestation of the earth and should be exterminated.
3. What species could be argued to be superior to humans and by what criteria?

29

There is no truth or falsehood and no purpose of life.

Truth is defined as that which is real or valid. There is scientific truth based upon observation and experimentation, historicity based upon credible and reliable sources, judicial truth based upon witness testimony and other evidence, spiritual truth based upon miraculous events, and subjective truth based upon personal experience.

As one considers the observable universe or one's immediate environment, there is an associated need to organize, understand, and make sense of every separate element or identifiable entity. There is a need to determine the usefulness of things depending upon the purpose deemed important to fulfill.

As one considers the purpose of any object, emotion, or thought, there emerges a need to include sensory information in order to reach conclusions for this insatiable, constant, and obsessive characteristic of humans.

The ultimate purpose being asked is concerning, "What is the meaning of my life or why do I exist?" and "Why does the universe exist?"

The ability to create or invent a purpose for things, including human life, is something for which the human species is especially known. The purposes and conclusions about observed objects, emotions, and thoughts, then become truths.

As one observes oneself and the world and the universe, one possible purpose of human life is to be accountable for behaviour. Other suggested purposes are: to evolve, to procreate, to exercise intelligence and creativity, to experience human qualities, and so on. Humans assign value to conclusions and purposes in terms of right or better or workable or equal but different, and so on.

A Roman governor once asked, "What is truth?" in reply to a man on trial who said he came in order to testify to the truth (John 18:37). If there is no God, there is no truth because there is no source of spiritual knowledge for essential conclusions about life.

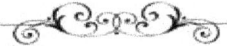

Thought Questions

1. How is the truth about anything determined?
2. What is the difference between subjective and objective truth?
3. If there is no God, how is the purpose of human life to be determined?

30

Art and beauty are illusions.

The broad definition of art is anything perceived with any of the senses or even imagined and subjectively regarded as having beauty, design, or meaning. Art is found occurring in nature in rocks and spider webs, and it is also found it the creative efforts of humans. All human art is a replication of form and design found in nature from naturalism and realism to impressionism, surrealism and post-modernism.

It has been said, "Beauty is in the eye of the beholder." This refers to the subjective or personal view of the individual who regards a thing or a thought or even an emotion.

In other words, art is anything perceived by a single human. What is artistic merit or the quality of art that makes it art? It is only human perception. Whatever a human perceives or experiences is art: a leaf, an atom, a rock, a thought. Therefore art is individual subjective human experience, and it may be argued that there is nothing that is not art.

As to its basic constitution, art is a spiritual idea having no scientific foundation. From this viewpoint if there is no God, art is an illusion of the human animal. Beauty is subjective, and that which is subjective is an illusion although there is much that is created and organized within this illusion.

At best, the reality of subjective perception is only individual, but as applied to humans generally, subjectivity has no definite proof beyond what one hopes in order to satisfy the pain of loneliness that would result from the belief that others do not share common human perceptions.

Art is one of the essential qualities of God who saw all that he had made, and it was very good (Genesis 1:31). Humans are made in the image of God and possess this same quality of creativity, only because God spoke it.

Thought Questions

1. What is creativity?
2. Why are only humans able to be creative?
3. Why is creativity essentially spiritual in nature?
4. Who defines what is art?

31

There is no music above noise.

Music is a peculiar and arbitrary human belief, without any objective reality. One person's music may be another person's noise and vice versa. Music can be heard in the sound of wind, birds chirping, rustling leaves, and baby's cry. Perhaps the idea of music can be broadly defined or discarded altogether as an individual and indefinable preference.

Classical and modern categories of music composed by humans range from what some call primitive by their own standards such as a drumbeat, to a composition involving many instruments, players or singers coordinated in parallel and harmonizing strains as performed by orchestras, choirs, and operas.

Is there a universal sound created by humans, which is regarded by all as appealing, satisfying, or entertaining? One observation seems clear: that it is common among humans to create sounds with some organization for the purpose of expressing something that reflects the emotions or passion of the human personality or soul.

This human organization of sounds involves some kind of repeated rhythm or extending a sound or note often in combination with other extended sounds.

However, the possible variations of these human sounds appear to be so numerous, that nay attempt to define music beyond this seems impossible. Human music then is a combination or set of random or organized sounds intended to express human emotion, and as such they are part of the human delusion or fantasy produced by human creativity.

The value of music as distinguished from any other noise is affirmed by a divine instruction to be filled with the Spirit by means of making music in one's heart to the Lord.

Thought Questions

1. How is music distinguished from any noise made by animals or objects?
2. Who defines what is music?
3. What is the spiritual nature of music?
4. How is music related to creativity?

32

There is no winning or losing or achievement.

Sports activities have been exciting and important for millions of people. The thrills of the game, the triumph of winning, and the nobility of losing with dignity and grace, are values and perspectives shared by those who compete against themselves and others. For many humans, sporting activities give significant meaning to life.

Yet what does it mean to win or lose? These ideas and values are purely arbitrary beliefs, which again illustrate the peculiar nature of the human animal. The physical and psychological benefits of sports are predicated on the more basic belief in the value and purpose of human life.

Sporting activity is shallow and meaningless. Moving small figures on a chessboard and in a particular way, demonstrates that one person is more or less clever than another, keeps the mind sharp, or perhaps contributes to social skills and interaction. Yet the idea of cleverness has no real value if human intelligence is purely evolutionary and unrelated to God.

The phenomenon of sport and the game, while there is little rational explanation of its value, seems to meet other delusional human needs for imagined achievement and self-worth. Competing and winning or losing, appear similar to human dreams during the sleep state in which there is a momentary sense of emotional excitement accompanied perhaps by the imagined admiration of or disappointment in self or others, but that soon passes upon waking.

All physical striving and advancement of human virtues and strengths, are of no worth unless they are directed toward the divine goal which is the foundation of all human existence: love for God and his love for mankind showing us how to love others.

Thought Questions

1. What does it mean to win, to succeed, or to fail?
2. What is the value of human achievement and who defines this value?
3. Why is it important to try hard at anything?

33

There is no difference between material and non-material.

A widely accepted notion is the distinction between that which is tangible or material and that which is intangible and unseen? Love, hate, and indifference are not physical, yet few would deny they are real.

The emotions and the virtues are real from a human viewpoint, and their distinction from the material is an arbitrary one. It would be just as valid to say they are tangible and material.

The distinction between material and non-material reality is a human creation. The material is observed with the five human senses. Yet when a human dies and is no longer able to sense the physical, other humans continue to observe and to believe in physical reality based upon observation.

The physical universe does not exist but is rather a unique concept of humans. The physical universe contains self-awareness because this is a human ability, humans being part of the universe.

God, who is conceived to be non-material, may be defined as that which is greater than the sum of the whole, including self-awareness since this is part of humanity. Everyone has the knowledge or sense of self-awareness or self-identity, yet that it is not considered to be physical seems quite arbitrary. Although not physically observable, self-awareness is a subjectively experienced reality as concrete as anything perceived by physical senses, and corroborated by the reader at this moment.

The barrier between the material and the non-material is therefore an artificial human idea or belief with an inherent bias against the existence of the spiritual. If God does not exist, self-awareness is part of the non-material human delusion and nothing more.

Thought Questions

1. Who defines the difference between what is material and non-material?
2. What is intangible or non-material yet exists?
3. How is the distinction between things material and non-material an arbitrary matter?

34

There is only nothing.

There is only nothing because there is no love or indifference, no meaning or nonsense. None of those perceptions associated with human awareness, have any value or reality or existence beyond the gas and dust of the universe.

The concepts of value, reality, or existence, are human oddities like the migration of butterflies, the mating rituals of birds, the hibernation of bears, and the orbits of comets and asteroids. To believe that these have significance or meaning, is futility. They are simply particular organizations of atoms, and human thoughts are merely electrons traveling along nerve cells, nothing more.

The existence of matter and energy are of no real consequence. The ideas about reality exist only in the minds of human beings. The absence of matter and energy is of no greater importance than their existence.

The further implication is that since only nothing is important or of value, this is to say also that only nothing exists. The reality is also that nothing has value or importance, since the concepts of value and importance are purely abstract human beliefs and not observable material scientific facts.

A vacuum is sometimes defined as nothing, but it is also defined that anything that has no value or importance is also nothing in the sense that it has no value of any kind. Therefore, only nothing exists. The value, reality, and existence of anything rest only upon the belief that God does exist. Divine existence gives value to all things, but only if one believes.

The distinction between something and nothing is an arbitrary human boundary and an abstract concept. The idea of "something" as referring to value is a belief since nothing can also be ascribed as much value with as much validity as ascribing value to something.

For example, if there is no war, there is peace yet peace does not exist as something. Rather peace is the absence of war, yet although peace does not exist and is nothing, it is assigned great value.

Human love and virtues exist as nothing, yet they are believed by many to have great value. Without God, these unseen qualities of great value, would not exist beyond the realm of human delusion.

Thought Questions

1. How is something to be defined and distinguished from nothing?
2. How is the existence of anything, actually a subjective conclusion or belief?
3. What unseen things are believed to exist yet only as subjective individual experience?
4. If there is no God, how can it be argued that anything has value, and therefore is something rather than nothing?

35

Something is nothing, and nothing is something.

The distinction between something and nothing is an arbitrary belief and without scientific proof. In fact, it can be understood that nothing is something because if nothing were not something, nothing would not exist.

Nothing is something. Otherwise, nothing would not exist. If nothing does exist, nothing is something. If nothing does not exist then there is no such thing as nothing. If there is no such thing as nothing, only something exists. If only something exists, it cannot be distinguished from nothing. If something cannot be distinguished from nothing, then there is no reason to affirm that something exists; something can be affirmed as nothing.

Something exists however only because it is in contrast to nothing. If there is no such thing as nothing, then the concept of something is meaningless. Something is defined as that which exists. If that which exists, is defined as what can be perceived by one's own senses, then the thoughts, emotions, and perceptions of other people, are nothing or do not exist.

Whatever one perceives, is subjective and is ultimately alone and without corroboration. And corroboration does not exist because it is the subjective report of another person. While one may affirm that existence is a reality, human knowledge of the existence of reality, although assumed by the human child from his first awareness, depends upon belief.

By divine revelation we are able to believe that there is something or that anything exists: In the beginning God created the heavens and the earth (Genesis 1:1). By these words, a foundation is given for believing the existence of something: time (beginning), being (God), intelligence (created), space (heavens) and matter (earth).

Thought Questions

1. Why does nothing have to be something?
2. Why is something also nothing?
3. Do human memory, thought, and emotion exist if they cannot be observed?
4. If perception is subjective, how can it exist as something if others cannot observe that which is subjective?
5. How is asserting that anything exists or is something, based on belief?

36

There is no meaning,

and meaning is an illusion.

The famous atheist Bertrand Russell said, "Unless you assume a God, the question of life's purpose is meaningless." Indeed, all questions, all human activity, and all things are meaningless.

Unlike the activity of animals and plants, the idea of meaning refers uniquely to the activity of humans to think or reason, to know and understand, and to communicate. Meaning refers to purpose or function, to the explanation of something about which humans think.

The purpose of a tree is not to make oxygen any more than its purpose is to grow or to die and become dirt. If there is no God, meaning is irrelevant because meaning is only a peculiar activity of human thought.

Plants and animals and inanimate objects do not consider meaning. They do not consider anything but simply respond to stimuli that affect their survival.

Humans have a propensity for establishing meaning to life and to every thought, every action, and to everything. Yet this is a futile and meaningless illusion, if there is no

God. For example, work and pleasure may serve to diminish pain and discomfort, unless these are pleasurable, and to increase stimulation of the senses. Yet these activites seem limited and shallow if there is no purpose or aim beyond themselves.

One may conclude that limited purpose, e.g. momentary pleasure, is sufficient and a meta purpose is unnecessary. Further, the notion of meaning or purpose may be irrelevant to existence: "It doesn't have a purpose. It just is." This statement however makes the point that there is only existence without meaning or purpose. Without meaning or purpose, the foundation of human life, its direction and motivation, are lost and confused.

If there is a God, the meta purpose of individual human life is established as well as the purpose of relationships with others, with the creation, and with the Creator.

Thought Questions

1. Explain why you think non-human animals do not consider the meaning of life?
2. What is your idea of the meaning or purpose of human life?

3. What alternative is there to thinking about anything having a meaning or purpose?

37

There is no justice or injustice.

What does it matter if a man murders, steals, or defrauds? If laws against these are intended to maintain order in society, this assumes order is good. Perhaps disorder and chaos are better because they provide an environment for the survival of the fittest or the strongest and the most clever. In fact, laws and imposed order are deleterious because in protecting the weak they enable the feeble to flourish thereby inhibiting the natural process of evolution through natural selection.

In the absence of God, there is no justice because justice demands a law or a standard of conduct. Based on natural selection, the law would exclude compassion or protection for the weak. Rather, natural selection would render unjust and immoral any system or conduct that enables weakness to persist or to drain the resources of society.

The weak would with justification be exterminated. Whatever race or condition was deemed inferior or devolved, would be marked for elimination so that the superior could thrive. The virtues of love, patience, gentleness, and meekness would be seen as weakness and condemned as crimes against the evolution of humanity.

The clever thief, liar, or murderer would be regarded as superior because of his ability to thrive, to amass wealth, to spawn offspring, and to rise to a position of power. Material achievement would define justice, and all compassion, service, and humility would be worthy of death.

Thought Questions

1. What has right and wrong to do with justice?
2. If there is no God, how is ignoring the needs of the poor an act of justice?
3. How could one justify extermination of the weak examples of human beings in society?

38

There is no reason or knowing or wisdom.

There no reason or knowing or wisdom, as anything more than peculiar features of human neurological processes. The obsession of humans is to find reasons, causes, explanations, and to identify effects. These human activities are vulnerable to individual subjectivity. That which is experienced as pain, can be interpreted as positive or pleasurable and vice versa.

That which is considered as something known depends upon individual human sensory perception. Something considered to be known, can only be known to one person: the one who knows or observes a thing.

One cannot know whether or not another knows something, and vice versa. Therefore, no one can know anything except subjectively. Subjective knowledge cannot be verified or demonstrated, because no one can know that others know. For something to be demonstrated, it must be demonstrated to someone.

That which is considered wisdom based upon what is practical and workable when applied to human experience, lacks any objective or observable standard. For example, killing another person may be practical because one's purpose is to remove an obstacle to self-advancement.

Without a standard, there is no wisdom whereby a concept, process, or judgment, can be assessed as wise. That which is considered wise by some because it increases the powerful, may be considered unwise by others because it decreases the weak. That which is considered wise because it exterminates the weak, may be considered unwise for the same reason.

All wisdom is based upon human assumptions and beliefs. For example, the wisdom of a person or group may be that marital fidelity is the happiest choice in a relationship given there is mutual attraction, respect, and commitment. This wisdom may hold that infidelity, even if both parties agree to an open arrangement, leads to jealousy and conflict, loss, grief, and unhappiness.

Another perspective is that infidelity could be redefined as true loyalty or fidelity to self and become the norm. In other words, if society or individuals released themselves from emotional pressures by accepting multiple sexual partners as normal, "infidelity" could be regarded as a wise and healthy choice.

Knowing and wisdom are based upon belief for the fear of the Lord is the beginning of wisdom (Psalms 111:10).

Thought Questions

1. Describe a meta principle for wisdom and knowing.
2. Why is knowledge subjective?
3. Why is belief necessary to determine wisdom?

39

There is no altruism.

Altruism is based on a belief in the value and worth of other humans to the extent that one is concerned about their welfare above that of self. Altruism also contains the belief that humans are of greater worth than non-human animals or objects. In the absence of God, there would be no reason for altruism.

Altruism requires three significant beliefs: other humans are of greater value than other animals or objects, the welfare of humans is more important than the well-being of other animals and objects, and the welfare of other humans is more important than oneself.

A belief, assumed by non-theists, is that altruism as a higher principle, is necessary for the continuation of the species and as such is linked to the instinct of survival, self-preservation, and protection of offspring. If we were selfish, we would not pay taxes, provide an inheritance for our children, purchase insurance, or pay proper wages to employees. If we did not do these things for others, we would place our own welfare in jeopardy.

However, therein lies the fallacy of the argument for true altruism does not care for its own welfare but only for the welfare of others. Self-interest as an ulterior motive of caring for others, negates the meaning of altruism. Self-sacrifice is the root of altruism whose only foundation is selfless love, beyond any explanation of scientific observation other than divinity: This is love, not that we loved God, but that God loved us, and sent his Son to be the sacrifice for our sins (I John 4:10).

Thought Questions

1. If there is no God, what is the basis of altruism?
2. Why would one desire to die to save the life of someone else?
3. If love is a basis for altruism, how can love be established or defined in the absence of God?
4. Without God, why is selfless love or altruism a delusional human characteristic?

40

Self-awareness and personal identity are self-delusions.

There is no who or self or others. The idea of who is a concept by and for humans to set them apart from other animals and life forms. Therefore, the idea of "who" is an arbitrary belief of humans "who", for example, do not regard plants and bacteria as "who."

Awareness of self is a sense of having an identity based upon perception through the senses, emotional experience, and the ability to engage in thought processes. Self-awareness is not limited by the loss of sight, touch, smell, hearing, or taste, since it continues with the ability to think and to feel emotion.

The awareness of oneself however is limited to oneself because one cannot be aware of the existence of others beyond believing that others exist. If there is no God, the sense of self is shallow, having no reality beyond that of the individual. Self-awareness is a peculiar quality of the human animal perhaps only somewhat more complex than that of other species and certainly not necessarily unique although the self-awareness of others cannot be proven scientifically.

Any belief that self-awareness makes one special or important, is a delusion. Since I am the only one whom I know to have self-awareness, how can I be sure I am real. There is no one who can verify my existence, only my own thoughts and emotions.

The French philosopher Descartes attempted to establish his individual existence based on his own self-awareness. His famous statement is: "I think, therefore, I am." What he failed to consider is that his ability to think, is itself a shared delusional process with which he and the human species are obsessed.

Even if self-awareness is true, it has no value or importance when separated from spiritual beliefs, since the idea of value is itself a spiritual belief. The belief that self-awareness is real and not a delusion is founded solidly on the spiritual call to love the Lord your God with all your heart (emotions), and with all your soul (spiritual), and with all your mind (thoughts), and with all your strength (physical) (Matthew 22:37). These parts define the sum of our individual identity and our capacity for self-awareness.

The existence of God can be extrapolated from the self-awareness, intelligence, and creativity of humans. The universe contains self-awareness, intelligence, and creativity because humans possess these qualities.

The universe shows broad evidence of creative intelligence and design. Since the whole contains the sum of all parts, it is reasonable to conclude that "God" is that which is greater than the sum of all parts, including self-awareness, intelligence and creativity, the great power behind the unlimited complexity of the universe. To find God, we need only look into the fundamental qualities of humans who are mirrors and reflections of God and made in the divine image.

Thought Questions

1. Why is an animal not referred to as "who"? For example, one would not say "a bird who flies" but rather "a bird that flies."
2. Why do you believe self-awareness is real and not simply a delusion?
3. How can you *prove* to anyone that you possess the ability to perceive your own existence if you do not know whether or not others have the ability to perceive their existence?

41

Other people do not exist.

The existence of other people is based on the belief that other people have self-awareness. There are observable signs that other people have self-awareness, but since one cannot experience or see the self-awareness of another, there is no direct proof of their existence.

One can hear others talk and respond. One can see and hear others cry or laugh, eat, walk, sleep, and engage in activities similar to one's own. However, one lacks the ability to experience or directly observe the actual self-awareness of others.

In this regard, the existence of other people is similar to the existence of God who, although not directly observed, is believed to exist because of the observable signs in addition to reason, for example, creative design in the physical universe, the necessary value of humans and morality.

Self-awareness by definition is subjective, which means it cannot be objectively or directly observed by anyone other than the individual possessing it. This means further that whatever cannot be observed, is unscientific and therefore is based on belief, not fact.

The existence of other people is based only on the belief that one should love one's neighbor as much as one loves oneself (Mark 12:31). This belief alone raises the value and therefore the existence of other people to a level equal to that of oneself. It is by this love that God is known and by which we know others.

Thought Questions

1. What is the difference between "knowing" and "believing" that other people exist?
2. What are the signs that others exist?
3. What are the signs that God exists?

42

Humans are a vermin parasite infestation of the earth.

Scientific reason requires that humans are by definition a vermin parasite infestation of the earth and eventually perhaps of the universe. A strong case for this is in the following well-known facts.

Humans are over-populating the earth. Humans are exploiting and destroying the forest habitats of thousands of species resulting in their rapid extinction. Humans are polluting and toxifying the atmosphere and water of the earth thereby altering the climate and threatening the ecosystem required by other species to survive.

Humans are producing increasing volumes of waste destroying the ocean habitat and its life forms. The human organism is exploiting and destroying other species for its own consumption.

If there is no God, humans should be subject to the same definition of infection, parasite, infestation, and vermin, as other species such as bacteria, viruses, termites, rats, maggots, and ants. Further, as an infestation humans should at least be culled when their numbers grow excessive or exterminated when they become a threat to the earth's viability or to the survival of other species. This extermination of humans should be applied at least locally if not globally as a noble virtuous act and a moral obligation by an "altruistic" hero willing to step forward.

On the other hand if there is a God, humans should be understood as creative beings having a free will to choose between right and wrong and given unique responsibility to care for the earth. As souls having individual moral accountability, humans should be judged individually and held responsible for their destructive acts upon the environment. This view of humans rests solely upon a belief derived from divine revelation, against the scientific naturalistic approach that would reasonably and with consistency, view humans as vermin and nothing more.

Thought Questions

1. Do you believe humans are a threat to the earth as a habitat for other species and life forms?
2. Do you believe humans are individually morally accountable or to be regarded as an infestation to be culled or exterminated?

3. What is the scientific definition to identify and explain behaviour of one species destroying the habitat of other species, and what is the scientific solution?

4. What is the spiritual definition to identify and explain human behaviour destroying the habitat of other species and what is the spiritual solution?

43

Life is useless.

Life has no value because the idea of value and worth is simply part of the need for belief characteristic of the human species. There is no standard for value and worth that would allow intrinsic value of any degree to be assigned to human or non-human life.

There is no real distinction between life and non-life because that which is real or true is part of a peculiar human neurological process. The idea of usefulness is understood in terms of what promotes survival of the species. The value of survival of a species is part of the peculiar thought process of humans and without any transcendent or metaphysical reality.

Life has no intrinsic value or meaning. If one insists that the meaning of life is to be fully human or to fulfill one's potential, the question becomes one of defining human potential. Perhaps it is to eat, grow old and die as any other animal. Perhaps it is to generate offspring and then die. Because humans are capable of killing and kindness, perhaps these should also be included.

In the absence of God or of any transcendent standard of priorities or values, there is no way to know whether the destructive abilities are to be controlled and the constructive abilities exercised. Perhaps the destructive abilities lend more to natural selection than do the constructive abilities. If so, one must assign the label "destructive" to certain choices and the label "constructive" to other choices.

The foundational principles for defining these criteria are missing, in the absence of divine revelation.

Thought Questions

1. If there is no God, what is the purpose and value of life?
2. Why do you not just end your life?
3. On the other hand, if there is a God, what is the purpose and value of life?

44

There is no reason to say thank you.

We express gratitude because we want to acknowledge or verbalize our appreciation for the act of kindness done for us by someone. To say "thank you" is believed to be considerate and polite; to recognize the gift or favour, generosity, and altruistic virtue of another demonstrated toward us.

"Thank you for giving me something that I did not possess on my own. Thank you for the act of consideration of my needs or simply for thinking of me or of someone I care about. Your consideration of me must have an ulterior motive."

Your apparently selfless act must in fact have to do with some advantage you are seeking for yourself. Perhaps you expect something from me, some favour or something in return. If not, you are a sick and deluded animal deserving of slaughter. If there is no God, I will say "thank you" and then plan a way to deprive you of your life and earthly possessions.

After all, there is no altruism, no truly selfless act. If one is deluded by the myth of kindness, it is a weakness to be eliminated because it undermines natural selection by enabling, supporting, and helping the weak to thrive rather than expecting the weak to survive by their own strength.

If there is no God, there is no ultimate source of all goodness to whom we direct our thanks, and any expression of gratitude directed toward impersonal natural forces would seem to fall upon deaf ears.

Thought Questions

1. What beliefs are implied by saying thank you?
2. Why should anyone believe you have his best interests in mind rather than your own advantage?
3. What emotions emerge inside you as you think that there is no one to thank for anything?

45

There is no reason to be polite and courteous.

Politeness is about showing courtesy, allowing others to go first, opening the door for others, helping them with their load, saying please, thank you and you're welcome. This courtesy and consideration for others, is based on the belief that other people have worth and dignity, that their worth merits kindness, and that kindness has value in itself requiring no other reward.

Without the spiritual, humans are reduced to practical value. In other words, rather than eternal souls, they are material objects with self-serving purposes of survival, comfort, and pleasure. Other human objects serve the purpose of one's own advantage. This perception of human value renders politeness irrelevant at least and at most a means to self-service.

Politeness expresses a high regard for human beings, for in the expression of gratitude, asking in place of demanding, allowing others rather than intruding, one recognizes and elevates the dignity, value, needs, and well being of others. In the absence of God who is the "father" of our spirits (Hebrews 12:9), the regard for all human beings and the foundation of altruism, kindness, and politeness, become meaningless and fade into absurdity and vanity. Self-interest in one's condition in this life only, becomes the highest norm. Rudeness and the law of the jungle prevail.

Thought Questions

1. What fundamental belief is courtesy based upon?
2. What fundamental belief is the foundation of belief in human worth and dignity?
3. If there is no God, what is the rationale for courtesy and polite behaviour?

46

There is no reason to trust.

Trust is based on the belief that time exists for it is about the future. Trust also requires the belief that others exist with like human qualities, that others can be relied upon for the future based on their past truthfulness or their pattern of conduct, and that others share a value in common with the one who places trust in them: the fulfillment of a task within the context of constancy and availability in a relationship.

Trust is more than predictability. One may predict that a person will cause harm to someone, and may say, "I can trust him to hurt me," which means I can predict that he will hurt me even though I do not want him to hurt me. This is a misuse of the word "trust" because trust by definition refers to a *shared* value.

Trust requires the belief that others have one's best interests at heart. In a world with no God, self-interest would be the norm. Any appearance of kindness would be dishonest because the ulterior motive of self-interest would always be present.

Natural selection encourages dishonest cleverness and trickery. Those who promote values of community and of the larger good, are in fact enabling the support of weak elements of the species.

Hitler and Stalin were consistent in their elimination of weak and threatening populations. Essential to the process was the institutionalizing of distrust by the instruments of their secret police. Distrust, suspicion, and reporting were given rewards, and secrecy, fear, and hiding became reasonable.

Thought Questions

1. What fundamental belief is trust based upon?
2. How would trust be affected in a society in which there is no belief in God?
3. How does belief in natural selection and survival of the fittest, affect the concept of trust?

47

There is no reason to hope.

Hope is by definition a belief in the future and in the existence of time. Hope may be based upon nothing but the desire for a future outcome, or hope may be based upon that which is both desirable and predictable based upon past performance. Hope based only on desire without predictability is blind hope.

Hope assumes life is worth living, that life has value, and that any achievement or human quality has value. Hope is about the future, but since the future cannot be observed, it is not an objective reality.

In other words, the future does not exist, and there is no such thing as the future. Humans hope only because they believe. Without belief, there is no hope because there is no future for which to hope.

Without hope, there would be no creativity, no planning, no art, no invention, and no human endeavor of any kind. Hope is a belief because it cannot be seen. The expectation of something positive that will happen may be based upon the evidence of things that can be observed or have been observed. Because of the evidence, one believes or trusts that the expectation will be fulfilled. The substance of hope is the element of belief or confident certainty or trust that goes beyond evidence.

In the absence of the spiritual, hope is shallow and confined to the ultimate despair of shallow material expectations. The spiritual element of hope reaches beyond the material, based upon the evidence that in light of all reasonable thought God must exist. The single truth of God gives value, meaning, and hope to life, without which there is only futile pointless effort.

Thought Questions

1. What beliefs does hope depend upon?
2. How is hope affected if there is no God?
3. How does hope relate to the future?
4. What has hope to do with belief in the value of life?

48

There is no reason to show honour, acknowledgment, and praise.

To honour, praise or compliment the behaviour of another is based upon the belief that others are worthwhile, that they are capable of receiving honor, and that their choices possess value. Sometimes honor is given as an example for others to show honor or to emulate behaviour that is honorable. This is based on the belief that it is worthwhile to instruct others in honorable behaviour.

The value assigned to behaviour deemed as honourable is arbitrary depending upon shared cultures and philosophies. Society honours those who contribute to human advancement or well being whether it is in the local school or government or an area of scientific understanding. Regardless of the field, the bestowal of honor and praise for well doing depends upon the value assigned by the group.

In the determination of what is honourable, the group must develop a spiritual element or belief. Humans often agree in large numbers on basic values such as achievements that contribute to the material welfare of humans or the environment.

This bestowal of honour may seem odd or irrelevant if one begins with the premise that since there is no God, there is no real value in preserving humans or the environment. The ritual ceremonies acknowledging achievement of anything or respect or regard for anyone, then seem absurd and peculiar.

To humans themselves, their rituals are sophisticated and advanced only because the associated value is believed to transcend the material world. In the absence of God, nothing is transcendent, but earth-bound and destined for dust.

Thought Questions

1. What beliefs does showing honour depend upon?
2. How does honour relate to human worth?
3. How is showing honour affected if there is no God?

49

There is no reason for service.

Service is based on the belief that the act of helping or assisting other human and non-human life, or causes of any kind, has value and importance. This service may be assigned valued based on its own fulfillment or expressed by others through some material reward or reciprocation. If there is no material reward, the value or motive in helping others may be purely one of altruistic desire based only on a belief in the virtue and attached emotional reward derived intrinsically from such acts of service regardless of reciprocation or acknowledgement from others.

Service arises from a desire to care for others. Why would anyone want to lower himself without remuneration or material reward? This is an irrational choice unless there is a spiritual motivation or reward. A society without service is a society without virtue.

Imagine a society in which people provide no kindness or service as an end in itself but always expect payment. Every time a courtesy is done, a hand is extended or a bill mailed to receive payment. This by definition would mean the end of courtesy.

On the occasion when Jesus washed the disciples feet, he did it to show the virtue in lowering oneself to perform a thankless task, and that it is considered the highest quality to serve others without reward. In washing their feet, Jesus also demonstrated his high regard for those he served. This is purely a spiritual belief expressing belief in the value of others who are served.

If there is no God, the foundation for such a belief is lost and the bedrock of service and compassion in society is made void replaced by a cold and selfish motive.

Thought Questions

1. What beliefs does service depend upon?
2. How is the definition of service affected if there is no God?
3. What is your definition of true acts of service and what beliefs are implied?

50

There is no mercy and no forgiveness.

    The concept of forgiveness requires a number of beliefs in addition to believing that other people exist and are worthwhile. Forgiveness depends upon the beliefs that it is good mental health to forgive others, that a sincere apology is a pre-condition to extending forgiveness, and that it is desirable to experience the peace that can result when forgiveness is offered and received.

    If there is no God, forgiveness is unreasonable and a sign of weakness. Rather vengeance, retribution, and punishment are the rule for any infraction or offense. Forgiveness of those who offend is to enable that behaviour, and is therefore deleterious to the evolution of the species. An apology and repentance are not enough to ameliorate the negativity of the offensive behaviour. There must be a penalty and a price to pay. Maiming and death would not be too extreme.

    There is no mercy, only vengeance. If you strike me, I will strike you back. If you kill my brother, I will kill you and your brother. There must be retribution. We must fight to the death, and may the strongest survive. This is the way of natural selection. Anything less will weaken the gene pool if the weak and their forgiving and merciful enablers are allowed to survive. Let those who beg for mercy be destroyed along with those who forgive them, for they are too weak to win by brut strength and wit.

The value of mercy and forgiveness is elevated only in the example of God who taught us to be merciful to everyone just as God is (Luke 6:36), and that God's people must practice compassion, kindness, lowliness, meekness, and patience, and be forgiving just as God is (Colossians 3:12,13).

Although we deserve destruction because of our offenses, God showed mercy and offered forgiveness. Only through this divine example first demonstrated to us, do we know the means and value of mercy and forgiveness. Without forgiveness and mercy, any society is thrown into the violent chaos and darkness of relentless vengeance seen during our own time in suicide bombing, terrorism, raging warlords, and tribalism.

Thought Questions

1. If there is no God, what is the basis of extending mercy and forgiveness to those who are truly sorry?
2. What would be the state of society without mercy?

3. How does mercy contradict and undermine the theory of natural selection?

4. Can you make a case for vengeance and retribution and against mercy and forgiveness as unscientific, illogical, and damaging?

51

No one has a right to live.

Of all the rights held dear by humans, the right to live is surely the greatest. If this right is not upheld, believed, defended and protected, then the life of every individual is threatened. Everyone becomes vulnerable to attack and death. The entire judicial system is founded upon this fundamental right, and from this right spring all other rights and freedoms extolled in a democratic and free society.

This right to life is taken for granted and assumed by most, yet it has no basis in science. The idea of a right in itself, is that a belief or value is assigned to some human activity such as speech or assembly.

The idea of the right to life is based upon the belief that human life has value. In the absence of God, human life has no value at all and certainly no greater value than objects, plants, animals, or euglena.

The defense of human life for the non-theist is predicated on self-preservation. The reasoning is that if one wants to live, he should uphold the right of others to live. This self-focused reason to uphold the right of others to live breaks down in situations of desperation. If one's own life is threatened because of lack of food, for example, one is then justified in stealing from others who may need the food to survive.

The idea of a "right" implies that it is something that should be recognized as true because it is a law or because it is guaranteed or granted by some authority.

In the absence of God, the only authority granting such a right would be human government. If government is the only authority, then government can make arbitrary exceptions as for example, Hitler who decided Jews have no right to live. Any individual with a self-defined superior agenda, can decide who should not live.

Only if the value of human life and the right to life are believed to be divine or spiritual truths, can we build a secure and just society.

Thought Questions

1. What beliefs do human rights depend upon?
2. Imagine what happens to human rights in a society in which there is no belief in God?
3. Why do you believe humans have a greater right to live than other life forms?

52

The painful emotions of humans are empty and trivial.

The painful emotions are based on the illusion that the associated event is important or exists: for example the death of another person believed to be intimate, a behaviour believed to be offensive, an object or event believed to be threatening, a personal event believed to diminish one's own worth, a behaviour believed to be wrong, or one's future believed to be meaningless.

Emotions are based upon a significant degree of subjective belief and are at the heart of human nature. Hormone changes in the body can contribute to one's vulnerability to emotions, but there is always an element of subjective perception, understanding, and belief.

A young person is happy about graduation because she believes there is value in working for and receiving the special piece of paper or the title "graduate."

A man kills his wife out of jealousy and hatred because he believes her having an affair and leaving him takes away something necessary to his life. A person commits suicide after bankruptcy and the prospect of going on welfare because he believes the loss of material possessions means he is a failure and that his life has no value.

Because emotions are based almost entirely on subjective belief, one must base his emotions on beliefs which have the most evidence to support them: joy based on belief in God and life hereafter; guilt, fear, and sadness based on belief in behaviour offensive to God.

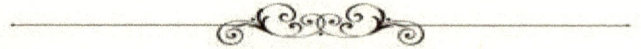

Thought Questions

1. If there is no God, what are the implications for human emotions?
2. What beliefs are human emotions based upon, for example: sadness, anger, guilt, fear, low self-worth, despair?
3. Imagine a society in which emotions are discouraged because they are unscientific. What would it be like?

53

Humans are only objects with complex delusions elaborated by emotions, creativity, thoughts and beliefs.

The life of every human person ends in the grave, and there is nothing of the individual or of personal identity that continues except in atoms and molecules absorbed as nutrients by plants and animals or taking the form of non-living matter. Humans are peculiar in their delusional tendencies, taking into account the limits of human research restricting an understanding of the inner life of other living and nonliving things.

The human preoccupation with art, literature, architecture, technology, and other creative endeavours, proceeds from the ability to organize choices based on imagination fulfilled through manual tasks. Thoughts and beliefs also emerge from the organization of choices and imagination that lead to religion and social values intended to preserve life and protect offspring.

Human emotions such as fear, anger, guilt, sadness, and despair, also motivate the development of beliefs and values for the purpose of protecting against the pain of the human emotions. The belief in an after-life helps defend the fear of death.

The rule of law and development of law enforcement, help defend against the fear of death, fear of loss of sustenance, the potential destructiveness of anger and greed, and to protect against the sense of despair by providing a guarantee of security. The emotion of guilt is necessary in order to preserve social order, and so social values and norms are incorporated into religion in order to bring the threat of divine punishment as a deterrent.

Humans are therefore simply a complex animated object with peculiar obsessions which although fundamentally delusional having no reality beyond the material, yet they serve the purpose of preserving and perpetuating human existence.

Humans who discard these characteristic delusional human obsessions and who break through to "reality", become a danger to themselves and others because they lack empathy, remorse, and regard for the worth of themselves and others. They are ultimately faced with the despair and emptiness of human existence and of any human effort, creativity, emotion, or thought.

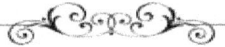

Thought Questions

1. If there is no God, what are the implications for human creativity?
2. Why are the unique qualities of humans either delusion or reflections of the divine?
3. If human qualities of thought and emotion are delusions, what are the implications for living?

54

Nothing is important.

No human thought, effort, or emotion has any value or importance. This is the only truth. The reason people do not want to think about this reality is because of the terror of facing nothing. This underlying terror is why people must resort to some belief system however irrational, because people need a reason to live, unlike other life forms or objects that need no reason to support their existence.

This nihilism, which was considered by the philosopher Friedrich Nietzsche, is the logical conclusion of the belief that there is no God. Nietzsche believed that the idea of God, is itself dead, and that this realization brought about by science, would result in the breakdown of all religions as well as social values and cultures. He thought that eventually mankind would gradually rebuild some new unknown value system.

Seen from this perspective, nihilism can be seen wherever traditional values based on theism are discarded, for example reflected in modern art and music, assisted suicide, the increase in serial and mass murder, genocide, and abortion that has occurred in modern times on an unprecedented scale. A further example is the legal acceptance of homosexual marriage, which never occurred even in ancient times, alongside the breakdown of the traditional concept of marriage and family.

Nihilism leads to increased pessimism, meaninglessness, despair, negativity, depression, suicide, and other forms of mental illness. We can see these trends occurring in modern society, and time will determine whether or not Nietzsche was correct or whether society will swing back toward strengthening convictions concerning the divine and therefore the intrinsic value of human life.

Perhaps the first words of scripture are intended to establish hope and to immediately dispel the despair of nothing: In the beginning, God created...

The awareness of the reality of God fills everything with meaning and value.

Thought Questions

1. Think about something important to you. What beliefs does the importance of anything depend upon?
2. What is nihilism and its implications?
3. If there is no God, how can the ultimate importance of anything be established?

55

This doesn't matter.

The concerns of humans to learn, to communicate, to write, to give birth, to form family units, to work, to achieve success and recognition, to contribute to human well-being, to save, to provide, to form societies, to observe laws, to pay taxes, are ultimately meaningless.

Whether to live or to die, or whatever one decides to do with life, is inconsequential. Whether the human species survives or not, deserves no consideration. Whether the earth or the universe continues or not, is not worthy of discussion.

The considerations reflected in this volume are of no importance. Any debate regarding the existence of God, is deserving of no interest but is understood as simply part of the relentless process of imaginative thought characteristic of that peculiar object self-styled as homo sapiens.

Perhaps happiness for a homo sapiens is to detach oneself from any interest in the meaning of life or in philosophy and religion, and to simply live as many attempt to do without thinking or considering the subject of this volume.

The other alternative is to fully adopt, develop, and indulge the human need to believe in the divine. In this way one becomes more fully human, not that it matters, except that one can perhaps be happy in his delusion rather than believing in nothing.

Thought Questions

1. Why is it important to think about the things written in this book?
2. Is the human desire to wonder about the meaning of life, only a peculiar feature of the human animal and nothing more?
3. If there is no God, how can the meaning or importance of the universe or of human life be explained?

Epilogue

But if God does exist, then............

Since everything requires a degree of belief or an aspect that is not objectively observable, one is left to decide what is true based upon the preponderance or amount and quality of the evidence. The *quality* of the evidence to establish the degree of probability of any truth is beyond the scope of this volume.

However, the reader may wish to research the models that have been developed by others in disciplines such as: the scientific method to establish a scientific fact, the judicial method in court proceedings for establishing truth, and the historical method for establishing historical fact.

The preceding titles for each meditation would be true if there is no God because each statement implies an essential element of spirituality. Indeed, the human experience of every part of life is spiritual and depends upon subjective belief or faith.

In order to establish the reverse of each of the chapter title statements in *Meditations On Believing,* the reality of a spiritual realm and ultimately the existence of a transcendent standard and authority, is a necessary underlying conclusion. Therefore, the existence of the spiritual and of God is demonstrated by reason alone as a logical necessity.

Bibliographic Reading List

Those who advocate a particular philosophy as well as those searching for their own, are best served by understanding the ideas of others who think differently and those who have given considerable thought to their own views. To encourage further reading and study, an extensive bibliography of both atheism and theism is provided in the pages that follow.

Bibliography of Atheism

Adams, Marilyn McCord and Robert Merrihew Adams, ed. The Problem of Evil. New York: Oxford University Press, 1990.

Alston, William. Perceiving God: The Epistemology of Religious Experience. Ithaca, NY: Cornell University Press, 1991.

Angeles, Peter. The Problem of God: A Short Introduction. Columbus, OH: Charles E. Merrill, 1984.

Angeles, Peter A. Critiques of God: Making the Case Against Belief in God. New York: Prometheus Books, 1976.

Banner, Michael C. The Justification of Science and the Rationality of Religious Belief. Oxford: Clarendon Press, 1990.

Bowker, John. Is God a Virus? London: SPCK Press, 1995.

Broom, Neil. How Blind Is the Watchmaker: Theism or Atheism: Should Science Decide (Avebury Series in Philosophy.) Aldershot, UK: Ashgate, 1998.

Buckley, Michael J., S.J. At the Origins of Modern Atheism. New Haven, CT: Yale University Press, 1987.

Camus, Albert. Neither Victims Nor Executioners. Philadelphia, PA: New Society Publishers, 1986.

Chambliss, J.J., editor. Philosophy of Education: An Encyclopedia. New York: Garfield, 1996.

Converse, Raymond W. *Atheism As a Positive Social Force.* New York: Algora Publishing, 2003.

Copleston, Frederick, S.J. *A History of Philosophy: Modern Philosophy: From the Post-Kantian Idealists to Marx, Kierkegaard, and Nietzsche.* New York: Doubleday Dell, 1994.

Darrow, Clarence. *Why I Am an Agnostic and Other Essays* (The Freethought Library.) Buffalo, NY: Prometheus, 1994.

Davis, Caroline Franks. *The Evidential Force of Religious Experience.* Oxford: Clarendon Press, 1989.

Dawkins, Richard. *The Blind Watchmaker: Why the Evidence of Evolution Reveals a Universe Without Design.* New York: Norton, 1987.

Dawkins, Richard. *The God Delusion.* Boston: Mariner Books (Houghton Mifflin), 2007.

Drange, Theodore M. *Nonbelief and Evil: Two Arguments for the Nonexistence of God.* New York: Prometheus Books, 1998.

Edis, Taner. *Is Anybody Out There? A Natural Atheology.* (preprint)

*Flew, Antony. *God and Philosophy.* London: Hutchinson, 1966. (See also Flew's book in the bibliography of theism.)

Flew, Antony. *God, Freedom, and Immortality: A Critical Analysis.* Buffalo, NY: Prometheus, 1984.

Flew, Antony and Alasdair MacIntyre. New Essays in Philosophical Theology. New York: Macmillan, 1955.

Flew, Anthony. God: A Critical Enquiry. Chicago, Ill: Open Court Publishing Company, 1984.

Fraser, Giles. Redeeming Nietzsche : On the Piety of Unbelief. New York: Taylor & Francis, 2002.

Freud, Sigmund [Strachey, James (Ed)] The Future of an Illusion. New York: Norton, 1975.

Gale, Richard M. On the Nature and Existence of God. New York: Cambridge University Press, 1991.

Gardner, Sebastian. Routledge Philosophy Guidebook to Kant and the Critique of Pure Reason. New York: Routledge, 1999.

Geivett, R. Douglas. Evil and the Evidence for God: The Challenge to John Hick's Theodicy. Philadelphia: Temple University Press, 1993.

Geivett, R. Douglas, and Brendan Sweetman. Contemporary Perspectives on Religious Epistemology. Oxford: Oxford University Press, 1992.

Hanson, Norwood Russell. "What I Don't Believe", in What I Do Not Believe and Other Essays, eds. Stephen Toulmin and Harry Woolf. Dordrecht, Neth.: D. Reidel, 1971.

Harbour, Daniel. An Intelligent Person's Guide to Atheism. London: Duckworth & Company, 2001.

Hegel, G. W. F., and Hodgson, Peter C., editor. Lectures on the Philosophy of Religion: Introduction and the Concept of Religion. Berkeley, CA: University of California Press, 1995.

Herrick, Jim. Against the Faith. London: Glover & Blair, 1985.

Hick, John and Arthur McGill. The Many-Faced Argument: Recent Studies on the Ontological Argument for the Existence of Go. New York: Macmillan, 1967.

Howard-Snyder, D. Evidential Argument from Evil. Bloomington, IL: Indiana University Press, 1996.

Hume, David. An Enquiry Concerning Human Understanding. La Salle, IL: Open Court, 1985.

James, William. The Varieties of Religious Experience. 1936. New York: Random House, 1994.

Joshi, S.T., editor. Atheism: a Reader. New York: Prometheus Books, 2000.

Joshi, S.T. God's Defenders: What They Believe and Why They Are Wrong. New York: Prometheus Books, 2003.

Kant, Immanuel. The Basic Writings of Kant. New York: Random House, Inc., 2001.

Kauffman, Stuart. At Home in the Universe: The Search for the Laws of Self-Organization and Complexity. New York: Oxford University Press, 1995.

Kierkegaard, Soren and Kierkegaard, Sren Kierkegaard's Writings. Princeton, NJ: Princeton University Press, 1991.

Krueger, Douglas E. What is Atheism? New York: Prometheus Books, 1998.

Le Poidevin, Robin. Arguing for Atheism: An Introduction to the Philosophy of Religion. New York: Routledge, 1996.

Le Poidevin, Robin, editor. Questions of Time and Tense. New York: Oxford University Press, 2002.

Lowith, Karl. Nietzsche's Philosophy of the Eternal Recurrence of the Same. Berkeley, CA: University of California Press, 1997.

MacIntyre, Alasdair, and Paul Ricoeur. The Religious Significance of Atheism. New York: Columbia University Press, 1969.

Mackie, J.L. The Miracle of Theism: Arguments for and against the Existence of God. New York: Oxford University Press, 1982.

Mackie, J.L. Ethics: Inventing Right and Wrong. New York: Penguin, 1977.

Masterson, Patrick. Atheism and Alienation: A Study of the Philosophical Sources of Contemporary Atheism. Dublin, Ireland: Gill & Macmillan, 1973.

Martin, Michael. Atheism: A Philosophical Justification. Philadelphia, Pa: Temple University Press, 1990.

Martin, Michael and Ricki Monnier, editors. The Impossibility of God. New York: Prometheus Books, 2003.

Martin, Michael. Atheism, Morality, and Meaning (Prometheus Lecture Series). New York: Prometheus Books, 2002.

Matson, Wallace I. The Existence of God. Ithaca: NY: Cornell University Press, 1965.

McCarthy, Gerald D., ed. The Ethics of Belief Debate. Dordrecht, Neth.: D. Reidel, 1983.

Messer, Richard. Does God's Existence Need Proof? New York: Oxford University Press, 1993.

Molnar, Thomas. Theists and Atheists: A Typology of Non-Belief. The Hague: Mouton, 1980.

Moreland, J.P. and Kai Nielsen. Does God Exist: The Debate between Theists and Atheists. Buffalo, NY: Prometheus, 1993.

Nielsen, Kai. Contemporary Critiques of Religion. New York: Herder & Herder, 1971.

Nielsen, Kai. Why Be Moral? Buffalo, NY: Prometheus Books, 1989.

Nielsen, Kai. Ethics Without God. Second edition. Buffalo, NY: Prometheus, 1989.

Nielsen, Kai. God and the Grounding of Morality. Ottawa: University of Ottawa Press, 1991.

Nielsen, Kai. God, Skepticism, and Modernity. Ottawa: University of Ottawa Press, 1989.

Nielsen, Kai. Skepticism. New York: St. Martin's Press, 1973.

Nielsen, Kai. Philosophy and Atheism: In Defense of Atheism. Buffalo, NY: Prometheus, 1985.

Nietzsche, Friedrich W. Beyond Good and Evil: Prelude to a Philosophy for the Future (1886). New York: Prometheus Books, 1992.

O'Connor, David. God and Inscrutible Evil. Lanham, MD: Rowman & Littlefield, 1997.

O'Hear, Anthony. Experience, Explanation, and Faith. London: Routledge & Kegan Paul, 1984.

Owen, H.P. The Moral Argument for Christian Theism. London: Allen & Urwin, 1965.

Parsons, Keith M. God and the Burden of Proof: Plantinga, Swinburne, and the Analytic Defense of Theism. Buffalo, NY: Prometheus, 1989.

Parsons, Keith M. Science, Confirmation, and the Theistic Hypothesis. New York: Peter Lang, 1990.

Penelhum, Terence. God and Skepticism. Dordrecht, Neth.: D. Reidel, 1983.

Phillips, D. Can Religion Be Explained Away?. New York: St. Martin's Press, 1996.

Phillips, D. The Concept of Prayer. New York: Seabury Press, 1981.

Phillips, D. Death and Immortality. London/New York: Macmillan / St Martin's Press, 1970.

Phillips, D. Faith and Philosophical Inquiry. New York: Shocken Books, 1971.

Phillips, D. Faith after Foundationalism: Plantinga-Rorty-Lindbeck-Berger: Critiques and Alternatives. Boulder: Westview Press, 1995.

Phillips, D. From Fantasy to Faith. New York: St. Martin's Press, 1991.

Phillips, D. Introducing Philosophy: The Challenge of Scepticism. Oxford, UK: Blackwell, 1996.

Phillips, D. Philosophy and the Grammar of Religious Belief. New York: St. Martin's Press, 1995.

Phillips, D. Religion and Morality. New York: St. Martin's Press, 1995.

Phillips, D. Religion and Understanding. New York: Macmillan, 1967.

Phillips, D. Religion Without Explanation. Oxford: Blackwell, 1976.

Phillips, D. Wittgenstein and Religion. New York: St. Martin's Press, 1993.

Pike, Nelson, editor. God and Evil. Englewood Cliffs, NJ: Prentice Hall, 1964.

Pinxten, L., R. Thibau, R. Apostel, F. Vandamme, editors. Religious Atheism: Philosophy and Anthropology. New York: Prometheus Books, 1981.

Plotkin, Frederick Faith and Reason. New York: Philosophical Library, 1970.

Prevost, Robert. Probability and Theistic Explanation. Oxford: Clarendon Press, 1990.

Rand, Ayn. The Virtue of Selfishness: A New Concept of Egoism. New York: Signet Books, 1964.

Ray, Matthew A. Subjectivity and Irreligion: Atheism and Agnosticism in Kant, Schopenhauer, and Nietzsche. (Ashgate New Critical Thinking in Philosophy.) Burlington, Vermont: Ashgate Publishing Company, 2003.

Rescher, Nicholas. Pascal's Wager: A Study of Practical Reasoning in Philosophical Theology. Notre Dame, IN: University of Notre Dame Press, 1985.

Robinson, Richard. An Atheist's Values. Oxford: Blackwell, 1975.

Sartre, Jean-Paul and Cummings, Robert D. The Philosophy of Jean-Paul Sartre. New York: Random House, Inc., 1972.

Schellenberg, J. L. Divine Hiddenness and Human Reason (Cornell Studies in the Philosophy of Religion). Ithaca, NY: Cornell University Press, 1993.

Shermer, Michael. How We Believe (2nd Edition): Science, Skepticism, and the Search for God. New York: W H Freeman & Co., 2003.

Smart, J.J.C. and J.J. Haldane. Atheism and Theism. Oxford, UK: Blackwell Publishers, 1996.

Smith, George H. Happiness in a Godless World. New York: Prometheus Books, 2004.

Smith, George H. Atheism: The Case Against God. New York: Prometheus Books, 1989.

Smith, Quentin. Ethical and Religious Thought in Analytic Philosophy of Language. New Haven, Conn: Yale University Press, 1998.

Sobel, J. Howard. Logic and Religion: Essays in Analytic Philosophy of Religion. Cambridge, UK: Cambridge University Press, (preprint).

Stenger, Victor J. Has Science Found God? The Latest Results in the Search for Purpose in the Universe. New York: Prometheus Books, 2003.

Sutherland, Stewart R. Atheism and the Rejection of God: Contemporary Philosophy and the Brothers Karamazov. Oxford, England: Blackwell, 1977.

Tolley, Edward P., Jr. Beach Blanket Atheism: The Beginner's Guide for the Non-Believer. Pittsburgh, PA: Sterlinghouse Publisher, 2003.

Von Hippel, Arndt. An Evolutionist Deconstructs Creationism. Bloomington, Ind.: 1stBooks Library, 2000.

Westphal, Merold. God, Guilt and Death: an Existential Phenomenology of Religion. Bloomington, Ind.: Indiana University Press, 1987.

Wilcox, Howard A.. Ethics Without God: Optimal Realism, A Science-Based Philosophy. Garberville, CA: McGilvra Brown Press, 1996.

Bibliography of Theism

Alston, William P., and Richard B. Brandt. The Problems of Philosophy. Boston: Allyn and Bacon, 1974.

Auer, J. A. C. Fagginger; Hartt, Julian. Humanism Versus Theism. Ames, IA: Iowa State University Press, 1981.

Balfour, Arthur James, and Perry, Michael W., editor. Theism and Humanism: The Book that Influenced C. S. Lewis. Seattle, WA: Inkling Books, 2000.

Barrett, William. Irrational Man: A Study in Existential Philosophy. New York: Anchor Books, 1962

Basinger, David. The Case for Freewill Theism: A Philosophical Assessment. Downer's Grove, IL: InterVarsity Press, 1996.

Basinger, David. Divine Power in Process Theism: A Philosophical Critique (Suny Series in Philosophy). Albany, NY: State University of New York, 1988.

Beaty, Michael D., editor. Christian Theism and the Problems of Philosophy (Library of Religious Philosophy, Vol 5) Notre Dame, IN: University of Notre Dame Press, 1990.

Beaty, Michael D. and Mark T. Nelson, editors. Christian Theism and Moral Philosophy. Macon, GA: Mercer University Press, 1999.

Brooke, John Hedley, editor. Osiris: Science in Theistic Contexts: Cognitive Dimensions (Osiris: Second Series (Cloth), Vol 16.) Chicago, Ill: University of Chicago Press, 2001.

Broom, Neil. How Blind Is the Watchmaker: Theism or Atheism: Should Science Decide (Avebury Series in Philosophy). Downers Grove, IL: InterVarsity Press, 2001.

Brown, Stuart. Philosophy of Religion: An Introduction With Readings. New York: Taylor & Francis Books Ltd, 2000.

Byrne, Peter. The Philosophical and Theological Foundations of Ethics: An Introduction to Moral Theory and Its Relation to Religious Belief. New York: Palgrave Macmillan, 1999.

Cahn, Steven M. and Shatz, David, editors. Questions About God: Today's Philosophers Ponder the Divine. New York: Oxford University Press, 2002.

Calaprice, Alice, editor. The Quotable Einstein, Princeton, NJ: Princeton University Press, 2005.

Carmona, Matthew R., and Moser, Paul K., and Copan, Paul, editors. The Rationality of Theism (Studies in Philosophy and Religion (Martinus Nijhoff Publishers), V. 19.) New York: Routledge, 1999.

Clack, Beverley and Brian R. Clack. The Philosophy of Religion: A Critical Introduction. Williston, VT: Polity Press, 1999.

Clark, Kelly James, editor. Philosophers Who Believe: The Spiritual Journeys of 11 Leading Thinkers. Downer's Grove, Ill: Intervarsity Press, 1997.

Clark, Stephen R. L. God, Religion and Reality: The Case for Christian Theism. London, UK: Society for Promoting Christian Knowledge, 1998.

Conti, Charles. Metaphysical Personalism: An Analysis of Austin Farrer's Metaphysics of Theism. Oxford, UK: Oxford University Press, 1995.

Conway, David. The Rediscovery of Wisdom: From Here to Antiquity in Quest of Sophia. New York: Palgrave Macmillan, 2000.

Craig, William L. and Mark S. McLeod, editor. The Logic of Rational Theism: Exploratory Essays (Problems in Contemporary Philosophy, Vol 24). Lewiston, NY: The Edwin Mellen Press, 1990.

Craig, William Lane. God, Time, and Eternity: The Coherence of Theism II: Eternity. Dordrecht, Neth: Kluwer Academic Publishers, 2001.

Craig, William L. and Quentin Smith. Theism, Atheism, and Big Bang Cosmology. Oxford, UK: Oxford University Press, 1995.

Craig, William L. The Kalam Cosmological Argument. London: Macmillan; New York: Harper & Row, 1979.

Davis, Stephen T. God, Reason and Theistic Proofs (Reason and Religion). Grand Rapids, MI: Wm. B. Eerdmans, 1997.

Davies, Brian. An Introduction to the Philosophy of Religion. Oxford, UK: Oxford University Press, 1993.

de Bary, Philip. Thomas Reid and Scepticism: His Reliabilist Response (Routledge Studies in Eighteenth Century Philosophy.) New York: Routledge, 2002.

Devine, Philip E. Relativism, Nihilism, and God (Library of Religious Philosophy, Vol 2) Notre Dame, IND: Notre Dame University Press, 1989.

Dombrowski, Daniel A. Analytic Theism, Hartshorne, and the Concept of God (Suny Series in Philosophy). Albany, NY: State University of New York, 1996.

Dore, Clement. Theism. Dordrecht, Neth: D. Reidel Publishing, 1984.

Durant, Will. Story of Philosophy: The Lives and Opinions of the World's Greatest Philosophers. New York: Simon & Schuster Books, 1967.

Evans, C. Stephen. Philosophy of Religion: Thinking About Faith. (Contours of Christian Philosophy) Downers Grove, Ill: InterVarsity Press, 1985.

Flew, Anthony. There Is a God: How the World's Most Notorious Atheist Changed His Mind. New York: Harper One (Harper Collins), 2007.

Ford, Lewis S. Transforming Process Theism. (Suny Series in Philosophy) Albany, NY: State University of New York Press, 2000.

Forrest, Peter. God Without the Supernatural: A Defense of Scientific Theism. (Cornell Studies in the Philosophy of Religion) Ithaca, NY: Cornell University Press, 1996.

Forster, Roger & Paul Marston. Reason, Science & Faith. Eugene, OR: Wipf & Stock, 2001.

Frost, S. E. Basic Teachings of the Great Philosophers: A Survey of Their Basic Ideas. New York: Anchor Books, 1989.

Gall, Robert S. Beyond Theism and Atheism: Heiddegger's Significance for Religious Thinking (Studies in Philosophy and Religion, Vol 11.) Dordrecht, Neth: Martinus Nijhoff Publishers, 1987.

Gay, Craig. The Way of the (Modern) World: Or, Why It's Tempting to Live As If God Doesn't Exist. Grand Rapids, MI: W. B. Eerdmans Publishing, 1998.

Geivet, Douglas and Brendan Sweetmar, editors. Contemporary Perspectives on Religious Epistemology. Oxford, UK: Oxford University Press, 1993.)

Glynn, Patrick. God: The Evidence: The Reconciliation of Faith and Reason in a Post-Secular World. Rocklin, CA: Prima Publishing, 1997.

Groothuis, Douglas. Truth Decay: Defending Christianity Against the Challenges of Postmodernism. Downers Grove, IL: InterVarsity Press, 2000.

Guthrie, Stewart Elliott. Faces in the Clouds: A New Theory of Religion. Oxford, UK: Oxford University Press, 1995.

Hall, James. Knowledge, Belief, and Transcendence: Philosophical Problems in Religion. Boston, MA: Houghton and Mifflin, 1975.

Hasker, William. Metaphysics: Constructing a World View (Contours of Christian Philosophy). Downer's Grove, Il: Intervarsity, 1983.

Hawking, Stephen W. A Brief History of Time: From the Big Bang to Black Holes. New York: Bantam Books 1988.

Hebblethwaite, Brian. The Ocean of Truth : A Defence of Objective Theism. Cambridge, UK: Cambridge University Press, 1988.

Hemming, Laurence Paul. Heidegger's Atheism: the Refusal of a Theological Voice. Notre Dame, Ind.: University of Notre Dame Press, 2002.

Howard-Snyder, Daniel, editor. The Evidential Argument from Evil. Bloomington, IND: Indiana University Press, 1996.

Hugel, Friedrich Von, Baron, Ll. D., D. D. Essays and Addresses on the Philosophy of Religion. London: J. M. Dent, 1933.

Hunter, Cornelius. Darwin's God: Evolution and the Problem of Evil. Port Angeles, Wash: Brazos Press, 2001.

Kretzmann, Norman. The Metaphysics of Theism: Aquinas's Natural Theology in Summa Contra Gentiles I. Oxford: Clarendon Press, 2002.

Kung, Hans. Freud and the Problem of God. (translated by Edward Quinn) New Haven, CT: Yale University Press, 1990.

Lennox, John. God's Undertaker: Has Science Buried God? Oxford: Lion Hudson, 2007.

Manson, Neil, editor. God and Design: The Teleological Argument and Modern Science. New York: Taylor & Francis, 2003.

McCord Adams, Marilyn and Robert M. Adams, editors. The Problem of Evil. (Oxford Readings in Philosophy) New York: Oxford University Press, 1994

Mill, John Stuart. Three Essays on Religion: Nature, the Utility of Religion, Theism. (Great Books in Philosophy) New York: Prometheus Books, 1998.

Miller, Ed L. Believing in God: Readings on Faith and Reason. New York: Prentice Hall, 1996.

Moreland, J.P., ed. The Creation Hypothesis. Downers Grove, IL: InterVarsity, 1994.

Moreland, J.P. and Kai Nielsen. Does God Exist: The Debate between Theists and Atheists. Buffalo, NY: Prometheus, 1993.

Morris, Thomas V. God and the Philosophers: the Reconciliation of Faith and Reason. New York: Oxford University Press, 1994.

Moser, Paul K., editor. The Oxford Handbook of Epistemology. (Oxford Handbooks in Philosophy) Oxford, UK: Oxford University Press, 2003.

Murphy, Nancey C. and Peter Forrest. Theology in the Age of Scientific Reasoning (Cornell Studies in the Philosophy of Religion). Ithaca, NY: Cornell University Press, 1993.

Murray, Michael J. Reason for the Hope Within. Grand Rapids, MI: Wm. B. Eerdmans Publishing Company, 1999.

O'Connor, David. God and Inscrutable Evil. Lanham, MD: Rowman & Littlefield, 1997.

O'Connor, David. Routledge Philosophy GuideBook to Hume on Religion (Routledge Philosophy Guidebooks.) New York: Taylor & Francis, Inc., 2001.

Pailin, David A. and Stewart Sutherland, editor. God and the Processes of Reality: Foundations of a Credible Theism. New York: Routledge, 1989.

Phillips, D. Z. and Timothy Tessin, editors. Philosophy of Religion in the 21st Century (Claremont Studies in the Philosophy of Religion.) New York: Palgrave Macmillan, 2001.

Plantinga, Alvin and James F. Sennett, editor. The Analytic Theist: An Alvin Plantinga Reader. Grand Rapids, MI: Wm. B. Eerdmans Publishing Company, 1998.

Plantinga, Alvin C. God, Freedom, & Evil. Grand Rapids, MI: William B. Eerdmans Publishing Company, 1989.

Plantinga, Alvin. God and Other Minds: A Study of the Rational Justification of Belief in God. Ithaca, NY: Cornell University Press, 1990.

Plantinga, Alvin, editor. The Ontological Argument From St. Anselm to Contemporary Philosophers. With an Introduction By Richard Taylor. Macmillan, London 1968.

Plantinga Alvin. Warranted Christan Belief. Oxford: Oxford University Press, 2000.

Plantinga, Alvin and Nicholas Wolterstorff, editors. Faith and Rationality: Reason and Belief in God. Notre Dame, IN: University of Notre Dame Press, 1983.

Prevost, Robert. Probability and Theistic Explanation (Oxford Theological Monographs.) Oxford, UK: Oxford University Press, 1990.

Rachels, James. Created from Animals: The Moral Implications of Darwinism. Oxford, UK: Oxford University Press, 1998.

Rescher, Nicholas. Pascal's Wager. Notre Dame, IND: University of Notre Dame Press, 1985.

Richmond, James. Faith and Philosophy. [Knowing Christianity Series] New York: J. B. Lippincott, 1966.

Richmond, James. Theology and Metaphysics. New York: Knopf Publishing Group, 1971.

Robb, J. Wesley. The Reverent Skeptic: A Critical Inquiry into the Religion of Secular Humanism. New York: Philosophical Library, 1979.

Rowe, William L. Philosophy of Religion: An Introduction. Florence, KY: Wadsworth Publishing, 1993.

Rowe, William L. and Wainwright, William J. Philosophy of Religion: Selected Readings. Fort Worth, TX: Harcourt College Publishers, 2001.

Sagi, Avi and Daniel Statman. Religion And Morality. (Value Inquiry Book Series 26.) Amsterdam, Neth: Rodopi, 1995.

Schlesinger, George N. New Perspectives on Old-Time Religion. Oxford: Clarendon Press, 1988.

Sire, James W. The Universe Next Door: A Basic Worldview Catalog. Downers Grove, IL: Intervarsity Press, 1998.

Smith, Nicholas D. and Woodruff, Paul, editors. Reason and Religion in Socratic Philosophy. Oxford, UK: Oxford University Press, 2000.

Swinburne, Richard. The Coherence of Theism. Revised Edition. Oxford: Clarendon Press, 1993.

Swinburne, Richard. The Existence of God. Revised Edition. Oxford: Clarendon Press, 1990.

Swinburne, Richard. Faith and Reason. Oxford: Clarendon Press, 1981.

Swinburne, Richard. Miracles. New York / London: Macmillian / Collier Macmillan, 1989.

Wainwright, William J., editor. God, Philosophy, and Academic Culture: A Discussion Between Scholars in the Aar and the Apa (Aar Reflection and Theory in the Study of Religion, No. 11) Atlanta, GA: Scholars Press, 1996.

Weinberg, Julius R. and Keith E. Yandell. Problems in Philosophical Inquiry, Volume 1: Theory of Knowledge. New York: Holt, Rinehart and Winston, 1971.

Wood, W. Jay. Epistemology: Becoming Intellectually Virtuous (Contours of Christian Philosophy) Downer's Grove, Ill: Intervarsity Press, 1998.

Yandell, Keith E. Christianity and Philosophy. Grand Rapids, MI: W. B. Eerdmans Publishing, 1984.

Yandell, Keith. God, Man, and Religion; Readings in the Philosophy of Religion. New York: McGraw-Hill, 1973.

Yandell, Keith. Hume's "Inexplicable Mystery": His Views on Religion. Philadelphia, PA: Temple University Press, 1990.

Yandell, Keith. Philosophy of Religion: A Contemporary Introduction. (Routledge Contemporary Introductions to Philosophy) New York: Routledge, 1999.

About the Author

Daniel Keeran lives with his wife Jennie in Vancouver, British Columbia, Canada. Born in 1947, he is the youngest of four sons and the father of Phoebe and Seth. A practicing psychotherapist since 1976, he is currently engaged in writing, research, and community awareness related to homelessness through the website www.homelesspartners.com founded by him and his wife.

He is a graduate of David Lipscomb University (BA, European History), the University of Kentucky (MA, Russian History), and Kent School of Social Work, University of Louisville (MSW, Clinical Social Work).

In 1985, he and his wife founded the Counsellor Training Institute that expanded to five cities in Canada.

He has also written *Healing Words: The Counsellor Training Course Manual*, *Personal Counseling Journal*, *Ancient and Medieval Baptismal Fonts*, and *Radical Christianity: Peace and Justice in the New Testament*.